LIVING
AMONG
LIONS

PRAISE FOR *LIVING AMONG LIONS*

"In all my years of ministry, rarely have I seen a more desperate time when we need courageous Christians to rise up. In *Living Among Lions* the Benham brothers provide a clear call for modern-day Daniels who will take a stand and refuse to compromise their faith. These two men live out this message, and I am proud to call them friends."

—Dr. Charles Stanley, senior pastor,
First Baptist Church, Atlanta

"This book is a realistic assessment of what Christians face in America: like Daniel, we now find ourselves in Babylon. What I particularly enjoyed about *Living Among Lions* is the interplay between the reality of today's PC culture and the biblical data that gives us encouragement and hope. Read this book, and then pass it along to other people in your life who need to be reminded that God does bless and help those who stand for truth, even at great personal cost. These two young authors, who have personally experienced outrageous discrimination for their convictions, now courageously encourage us to be faithful despite the cost."

—Dr. Erwin W. Lutzer, senior pastor,
The Moody Church, Chicago

"Imagine if William Wallace had a twin brother. David and Jason Benham are modern-day Bravehearts, leading a courageous charge against a rotting culture. When you have to live among the lions, the Benham brothers are the kinds of Christians you want as neighbors. Oh, and they can also bench-press a Buick."

—Todd Starnes, Fox News Channel

"As the winds of the culture continue to shift, David and Jason Benham continue to stand for truth. In this book the Benhams push the envelope further and encourage us to courageously fight for the values we hold dear, challenging us to lovingly engage the culture from a biblical perspective. Drawing on examples in Scripture, as well as personal experiences, they provide a blueprint for hope in what feels like a turning point for America."

—Benjamin Watson, New Orleans Saints tight end

"This is a terrific book, full of life, encouragement, humor, and practical wisdom. And it is vintage Benham brothers, inspiring every believer to lead the courageous life of a counterculture world-changer."

—Dr. Michael Brown, *Line of Fire* host and author, *Outlasting the Gay Revolution*

"The Benham brothers are the living embodiment of Spurgeon's legendary comparison of the Word of God to a roaring lion—'simply let the lion out of its cage and it will defend itself just fine.' In an era of perpetually smiley-faced wimps, the Benham brothers remind us that real masculinity includes courage of conviction."

—Steve Deace, Conservative Review contributor and talk show host, Salem Radio Network

"If I didn't know the Benham brothers personally, I might think they were fictional characters. Twins, who are best friends, next-door neighbors, business partners, and so committed to their faith and families that they've both been willing to leave million-dollar deals on the table in order to honor them. David and Jason are bold and faithful men who have maintained a standard of integrity and character the likes of which our world rarely sees. It's so uncommon, in fact, that it seems like fiction. I can only pray that my three sons will follow their example and live as fearlessly among the lions of our culture as our friends. As a mother of boys, I'm so grateful that the Benhams have chronicled their insight and personal legacy in these pages."

—Priscilla Shirer, author and teacher

LIVING AMONG LIONS

HOW TO THRIVE LIKE DANIEL IN TODAY'S BABYLON

DAVID AND JASON BENHAM

WITH ROBERT NOLAND

W PUBLISHING GROUP

AN IMPRINT OF THOMAS NELSON

Published in Nashville, Tennessee, by W Publishing Group, an imprint of Thomas Nelson.

Published in association with the literary agency of WTA Services, LLC, Franklin, TN.

Thomas Nelson titles may be purchased in bulk for educational, business, fund-raising, or sales promotional use. For information, please e-mail SpecialMarkets@ThomasNelson.com.

Unless otherwise noted, Scripture quotations are taken from New American Standard Bible®. © 1960, 1962, 1963, 1968, 1971, 1972, 1973, 1975, 1977, 1995 by The Lockman Foundation. Used by permission.

Scripture quotations marked CEV are taken from the Contemporary English Version. © 1991, 1992, 1995 by American Bible Society. Used by permission.

Scripture quotations marked ESV are taken from the ESV® Bible (The Holy Bible, English Standard Version®). © 2001 by Crossway, a publishing ministry of Good News Publishers. Used by permission. All rights reserved.

Scripture quotations marked HCSB are taken from the Holman Christian Standard Bible®, HCSB®. © 1999, 2000, 2002, 2003, 2009 by Holman Bible Publishers. Used by permission.

Scripture quotations marked NCV are taken from the New Century Version®. © 2005 by Thomas Nelson. Used by permission. All rights reserved.

Scripture quotations marked NIV are taken from the Holy Bible, New International Version®, NIV®. © 1973, 1978, 1984, 2011 by Biblica, Inc.® Used by permission of Zondervan. All rights reserved worldwide.

Scripture quotations marked NLT are taken from the Holy Bible, New Living Translation. © 1996, 2004, 2007, 2013 by Tyndale House Foundation. Used by permission of Tyndale House Publishers, Inc., Carol Stream, Illinois 60188. All rights reserved.

Scripture quotations marked NRSV are taken from the New Revised Standard Version Bible. © 1989 by National Council of the Churches of Christ in the United States of America. Used by permission. All rights reserved.

Scripture quotation marked KJV is taken from the King James Version. Public domain.

Italics added to Scripture quotations are the authors' own emphasis.

Library of Congress Cataloging-in-Publication Data

Names: Benham, David (Entrepreneur) author.
Title: Living among lions : how to thrive like Daniel in today's Babylon / David and Jason Benham, with Robert Noland.
Description: Nashville : W Pub., an imprint of Thomas Nelson, 2016.
Identifiers: LCCN 2015043970 | ISBN 9780718076412 (trade paper)
Subjects: LCSH: Bible. Daniel—Criticism, interpretation, etc. | Christianity and politics—United States. | Christianity and culture—United States.
Classification: LCC BS1555.52 .B46 2016 | DDC 261.0973—dc23 LC record available at https://lccn.loc.gov/2015043970

Printed in the United States of America
16 17 18 19 20 RRD 6 5 4 3 2 1

To the countless Christians who have stood courageously for their faith throughout history—who have faced lions and never backed down. Now is our time to do the same!

Their faith helped them conquer kingdoms, and because they did right, God made promises to them. They closed the jaws of lions and put out raging fires and escaped from the swords of their enemies. Although they were weak, they were given the strength and power to chase foreign armies away.

Some women received their loved ones back from death. Many of these people were tortured, but they refused to be released. They were sure that they would get a better reward when the dead are raised to life. Others were made fun of and beaten with whips, and some were chained in jail. Still others were stoned to death or sawed in two or killed with swords. Some had nothing but sheep skins or goat skins to wear. They were poor, mistreated, and tortured. The world did not deserve these good people, who had to wander in deserts and on mountains and had to live in caves and holes in the ground.

All of them pleased God because of their faith! But still they died without being given what had been promised. This was because God had something better in store for us. And he did not want them to reach the goal of their faith without us.

—HEBREWS 11:33–40 CEV

CONTENTS

CONTENTS

INTRODUCTION

GOD'S PEOPLE IN A *VERY* DIFFERENT COUNTRY

W E'RE LOSING EVERYTHING. OUR business . . . our personal savings . . . everything."

These were the disillusioned words spoken by Mrs. Barronelle Stutzman, a seventy-year-old, white-haired grandmother, as she held her husband's hand to steady her own. With tears in her eyes, she spoke to us following a meeting we attended. She had been sued by the attorney general of Washington State for standing by her Christian convictions. She concluded with "This is a different country."[1]

A different country. We knew exactly what she meant. Our nation is morphing and shifting away from its foundation laid by our founding fathers and the favor given by our heavenly Father. Mrs. Stutzman has not changed her values over the years, but her nation has.

"I'm a trash man now. Every morning I wake up before dawn and hit the streets, taking out the garbage," said Oregon resident

Aaron Klein. "I'm home with the kids and try to pick up odd jobs here and there to help Aaron with the bills," said his wife, Melissa, after closing their bakery when they were forced by the state of Oregon to pay fines for refusing to compromise their faith. "We don't even recognize this nation anymore," they said.[2]

We don't recognize this nation. It's another example: the Kleins have not changed their values over the years, but their nation has.

"Well, guys, I've served my city for years and truly miss the influence I was able to have on the young people of Atlanta. Although I was mocked and ridiculed by some in the fire department for believing in the Bible, I'm at peace knowing that I was faithful to God. What really hurts me is that America's children are growing up in a very different country than I grew up in," Kelvin Cochran, former fire chief of Atlanta, told us.[3] The mayor fired Kelvin for his beliefs.

A very different country than I grew up in. Kelvin hasn't changed his values, but his nation has.

"I still can't believe I was thrown in jail. Not only was I honoring God by refusing to issue same-sex marriage licenses, but I was upholding my oath to the Kentucky Constitution, which has clearly defined marriage," Kim Davis told us as the firestorm of controversy over same-sex marriage erupted after the Supreme Court declared state marriage laws (between a man and a woman) unconstitutional.[4]

Mrs. Davis hasn't changed—America has.

These are just a few of the conversations we've had with salt-of-the-earth, tax-paying, patriotic Christians. We've come to realize America is fast becoming something quite different than what she has always been.

A different country—a *very* different country.

In high school I (Jason) wrote Mark 14:50 on my baseball glove as a reminder to stand even if no one else did: "And they all left Him and fled." Mrs. Stutzman, the Kleins, Kelvin Cochran, and Kim Davis are people living that verse today, and it's quite real to them. For the first time in our nation's history, choosing to live faithfully for Christ actually costs something for those who choose to stand against the ever-shifting culture.

A STIRRING TO STAND

In our own challenge regarding biblical values, when the pressure came to "bow down," we were certainly tempted to give in (*Jason: More so with David than me, of course*), but by God's grace, like our new friends in the faith, we chose to stand.

The following stories are examples of what we have experienced in the months after HGTV canceled our reality-TV show. In our first book, *Whatever the Cost*, we detail the circumstances surrounding what became a media frenzy as a result of our public stand for Christ. In this book our goal is to move from that point to today, sharing all God has taught us.

Following the network's announcement, a banking entity that was one of our longest-standing clients in our foreclosure business promptly removed their listed homes from our inventory, as well as our franchisees'. A third-party vendor reached out to warn us. And within fifteen minutes of the call, the property pullout began. When we asked for an explanation, they gave us the ol' Heisman Trophy stiff-arm.

When the story became public, we had all of our properties back within eight hours—along with a personal apology from the bank's president. The backlash from Americans spoke loud and clear, and the bank listened. Still, we felt in a very real way how standing up for biblical values can burn you quickly and furiously.

Two months later we helped bring a faith-based movie production to our home city of Charlotte, North Carolina. The film had a larger budget than most Christian movies, and we were heavily involved with the filming. Our real estate company was also written into the script. After production began, the mainstream distributor realized our deep involvement in the film—as well as our real estate sign in some of the scenes—and pressured the producers to remove us from as much of the movie as possible.

At a business conference a representative for one of our clients walked up and told us, "I am afraid we'll lose business if I voice support for you guys." This man is a director at his company, has been our client for years, and has sold hundreds of properties with us. But he was genuinely afraid of the backlash he'd receive just for standing by us.

In Florida, as we walked through another client's office for a meeting, several people stopped working and closed their doors. Apparently, many of the folks in this large office embraced the media's portrayal of us. We had had a good working relationship with this company for years. But many of its employees now decided to keep their distance. We did our best to show Christ's love and grace to everyone. Interestingly, our host for the day happened to be a gay man. Before we left, we had the privilege to talk with him in the company break room, and he prayed to begin a relationship with Jesus!

Here are a few more examples of the phone calls we received:

"Guys, I'm really sorry, but we have to cancel the school assembly for next week. Once the school superintendent found out that you were the speakers, she immediately cancelled the event."

"I was just told to remove all of our business from your company. I can't give you the reason, but I think you guys know why. This just makes no sense to me."

"Thanks for serving us for so many years, boys, but our ministry can't afford the backlash we anticipate when the activists find out you work with us. We love you as brothers, but we need to create a little distance for now. I hope you understand."

Honestly, messages like those became the norm for us.

But here's the good news: since the battle cry in our previous book, we have been traveling the country, calling Christians to stand boldly for Christ. And we hear a rumbling, a stirring, among believers who are *not* willing to bow to the gods of culture, but who *are* willing to live faithfully for Jesus—whatever the cost. A new kingdom people are on the rise.

How amazing is that? Scary yes, but even more exhilarating! These convictional Christians—those who actually live according to the convictions of their faith—have the chance to be God's instruments of light pushing back the darkness in an hour of history that is exclusive to us. This is our time! History is being written right now, and we get to be on the front lines. (*David: This is where Jason usually says, "Booya, Gramma!"*)

The choice for us today is clear: bow before God or bow before men.

ENTER DANIEL

During that crazy time in our lives, we drew courage from a biblical character whose life we sought to emulate—courage to stand for what was right in a culture that rewarded people for doing the opposite. Daniel and his buddies became a source of hope and strength for us. So in this book, we want to share some of the truths we've learned from his life.

Daniel's friends had one choice: bow or burn.

Daniel himself had one choice: live a lie or die in the lions' den.

They all chose to remain firm in their faith—true to the convictions that defined their lives and glorified the God of their fathers.

In 605 BC their nation changed, but they did not.[5] Their surroundings shifted suddenly to an alien place—geographically, morally, and spiritually. *But they chose to remain unchanged, unaffected, and unashamed.*

The people of Judah, Daniel's homeland, had rejected God. They removed His boundaries, so He had to remove their blessings. Babylon arose and took many of the Jewish people into captivity. Daniel was among those taken from his homeland to Babylon. God did not spare him from exile. But years before, his heavenly Father had captured his heart. So when Daniel's nation changed, his relationship with God did not.

In Babylon, Daniel chose to remain faithful among the faithless, determined to live with conviction—whatever the cost. No matter how much life changed around him, his beliefs stayed strong. Daniel kept heaven's culture alive, even in a foreign land. While serving in the king's court and being tempted by a life of luxury, his conviction produced commitment, and his commitment turned into courage. He made up his mind not to defile himself with the food, fortune, or fame of this new land. Daniel chose to take the *mess* and make it his *message*. And his committed faithfulness brought God's covenant favor. As he and his friends embraced God's instruction, they enjoyed God's influence. So they rose to the top of Babylon's kingdom.

Then the world around them began to change yet again, no longer favoring their convictions and turning against them. But they did not give in. They stood with courage, and God's favor remained. When Daniel's friends chose to *burn* in the fiery furnace rather than *bow*, God brought them through the fire untouched by the flames. When Daniel chose to *keep his windows open* while he prayed, rather than hide his faith, God kept him safe as a lamb as he lived among lions.

Eternity's perspective proves these men right and upholds their decisions. Daniel and his friends refused to operate *strategically* or seek to survive in safety. Instead, they lived *supernaturally*, choosing to thrive in the Spirit. Daniel knew his God was the ruler over the realm of mankind, and the earth belonged to Him. Daniel's job was simply to live faithfully—even in the face of adversity. His life encourages us that no matter how dire circumstances may seem or how opposed to God our culture becomes, God is always in control. Whatever life throws our way, we will not just survive; we will thrive!

SOME LIGHT CONVERSATION

When have you ever heard someone going to bed ask, "Could you turn on the darkness so I can sleep?" No. Instead, we say, "Can you please turn the *light off*?"

Have you ever opened a closet door, watched all its darkness escape, fill the room, and overshadow the light? Never. Rather, the light from the room invades the closet and overcomes its darkness. That's just the nature of light. "The Light shines in the darkness, and the darkness did not comprehend it" (John 1:5).

So darkness is not the real problem today. The problem is the Light has been turned off. But for that very reason, this is the greatest time to be alive. Light always shines brightest in the midst of darkness. All we have to do is shine the Light!

We are filled with hope because the night is always darkest just before dawn.

> For His anger is but for a moment,
> His favor is for a lifetime;
> Weeping may last for the night,
> But a shout of joy comes in the morning.
>
> —PSALM 30:5

We have hope because we serve a risen King, and His name is Jesus. Right now, He is seated at the right hand of God with a host of angels around the throne calling out:

> "Holy, Holy, Holy, is the LORD of hosts,
> The whole earth is full of His glory."
>
> —ISAIAH 6:3

His glory fills the earth and all He has made. That includes you!

Daniel is with the Lord now. Paul has already run his lap in the race. Peter, James, and John—they have all gone before us and are no longer. But *we* are here now, and God has given us the awesome responsibility to be His light in all the earth. He reveals His glory through our faithfulness and obedience.

Although we have never been cast into a furnace or thrown into a den of lions, we do know what it's like to be "burned" on a national scale in a media firestorm and to feel the "roaring lion" of 1 Peter 5:8 on our heels, trying to devour us.

While catching a flight to Dallas to be guests on the *Glenn Beck Show*, we watched with interest the looks people in the terminal had on their faces when they saw our ugly mugs, which had been all over the news at the time. And there we were, sitting in the Dallas–Fort Worth airport, wolfing down dark chocolate as if a cocoa famine were coming. One man was standing along the wall, watching us as we were at our gate. He waited until no one was around, then hurried up to us and said, "Are you the Benham brothers?"

"Yeah," we replied.

Looking over his shoulders both ways, he said, "Thanks for standing!" Then he hurried off, looking right and left, to make sure no one saw him talking to us. We laughed to ourselves. Did that *really* just happen? Is it *that* bad in our country that someone feels threatened for just *talking* to a Christian who stands with conviction?

Honestly, what we're experiencing in America pales in comparison to what Christians around the world are enduring. Christians in America feel more pressure than persecution—but that might change given the rapid decline in culture.

Pressure is feeling the push of culture to stray from our faith. Persecution is feeling the pain of choices made as we stand for our faith.

We wrote this book for those who feel that closing the windows and keeping quiet (contrary to what Daniel did in Daniel 6:10) is the only way to live in safety. We wrote it for that man in the airport who made sure the coast was clear when he thanked us—and for the thousands just like him whom we have met traveling throughout this country over the past two years.

On one hand, we are tempted to say, "Come on, guys. Stand strong!" But we get it. We were also tempted to keep quiet and blend in before we took our stand. And now we see how many Christians feel this same pressure and simply don't know what to do. They are well-meaning people with good hearts. Yet they struggle to muster the courage and wisdom to stand strong against the rising current of resistance to God's kingdom.

Our dad is a pastor, and he has a great paraphrase he teaches that is gleaned from one of Matthew Henry's commentaries on the book of Amos about the temptation of remaining silent: "The prudence of the serpent demands silence in evil times. The prudence of the lamb demands we speak."[6]

What do you do when your company makes it clear that taking a biblical or even moral stance will cause you to be fired?

Where do you turn when you refuse to give in to cultural pressure, yet your biblical values could result in a lawsuit?

How do you act toward someone who decides to kick you out and censor your views while vehemently protecting his own rights to judge you and destroy your character?

How do you live faithfully when the temptation to deny

Christ seems so sensible and pragmatic? After all, you can live to fight another day, right?

That is exactly why we wrote this book. We have found many Christians in our nation—perhaps including you—who need more than just another rebuke for failing to stand. We need encouragement, strength, and biblical inspiration. We need to remember we are God's people and citizens of His eternal kingdom. In Christ we possess the highest calling and the greatest inheritance. We are the light that drives away the darkness. Even with the rise of our own Babylon, we can stand as Daniel did and make a difference.

So we wrote this book for brothers and sisters who have the potential to transform their world but instead may find themselves hiding in the shadows of fear and confusion. Such people need Daniel's example more than ever. He is the perfect role model for our generation. His conviction, commitment, and courage empowered him—not just to avoid hiding in the shadows of Babylon but also to shine so brightly that he *changed* Babylon.

That is why we structured the three parts of this book after the three great characteristics we see in the book of Daniel:

1. Conviction
2. Commitment
3. Courage

Daniel possessed these qualities, and he lived them out. As a result, God gave him incredible favor and supernatural power. Though he started as an enslaved exile, Daniel emerged as one of the most powerful men in the world. He did not merely survive in Babylon; he thrived. He did not conform to his world; he transformed his world.

The same is true for us. When we take hold of these values and practice them, God will transform *us* so that we, too, can transform our world. The beauty of this "Daniel paradigm" is that it does not beat us over the head with a standard we cannot attain. Rather, it meets us where we are and builds us into what we should be—from the inside out.

So we will first look at what was going on in the heart and mind of Daniel—his *conviction*. What were the internal values he held dear? How did he relate to God and view himself in a foreign culture? Where did he get his internal reservoir of strength to accomplish what he did? Part one will reveal the conviction that transformed Daniel's heart.

Once we've established his internal foundation, we will then look at the practical conduct Daniel built his life upon—his *commitment*. How did Daniel build his convictions into practical, day-to-day life? What kind of disciplines flowed out of his convictions? Part two will reveal the commitment that transformed Daniel's lifestyle.

Finally, we will check out the fruit of Daniel's conviction and commitment—his *courage*. How did Daniel mark Babylon forever? What kind of brave exploits actually changed his culture? Part three will reveal the courage that transformed Daniel's world.

THE GAME PLAN

As former pro baseball players, we like to use sports analogies to help us apply spiritual principles. Conviction needs commitment just as a baseball player's natural talent needs a solid work ethic. Gifted players who lack the discipline to work hard in the gym and on the practice field will not make it to the big leagues. Likewise, Christians gifted with new life in Christ often have no impact because they don't *"work out* [their] salvation with fear and trembling" (Philippians 2:12 NIV). That is, they don't translate their internal values into the external disciplines of a spiritual *lifestyle.* (For more on what this means, read Hebrews 12:11; 2 Peter 1:3–8.) They may have conviction but no commitment.

But after commitment there is one more level. A talented, hardworking baseball player must take his natural gifts and work ethic, step up to the plate, and have the *courage* to swing for the fences. It does him no good if, on game day, he only tries to avoid missing the ball. No one wins that way. He needs the killer instinct to go after the ball and swing hard! Daniel was exiled to Babylon, yet he did not allow disappointment to waste his talents. He honored his convictions and cultivated a committed lifestyle. Then, when he stepped up to Babylon's plate, he resolved to swing hard! He did not remain in the dugout; he took the field and played to win.

We cannot allow our convictions to be values devoid of discipline. Christians need committed lifestyles to embody their faith and give God something to use. But we cannot stop there. Commitment must become the courage to swing for the fences. God has called modern-day Daniels to transform their world.

This book is structured to inspire in you a spiritual life like Daniel's—a personal culture of faith that moves from conviction to commitment and from commitment to courage. Our prayer is that when you finish reading, the impression of Daniel's example will be forged into your soul.

First and foremost, this is a book about transformation:

+ the transformation of our inner person, which leads to . . .
+ the transformation of our practical lifestyles, which will result in . . .
+ the transformation of our world.

These are the principles that marked Daniel—a transformed man who was then able to transform his world. And these same principles will work for us today in our nation. They will take fearful people like the man in the airport and turn them into champions. The time is now for a generation of modern-day Daniels to rise up and stand strong.

Yes, we now live in what has become a *very* different country, as did Daniel. But also like Daniel—by the grace of God—we can live among lions, thrive in Babylon, and transform our world.

AMERICA: A NATION CHANGED

*In those days there was no king in Israel; everyone did what
was right in his own eyes.*

—JUDGES 21:25

 When the celebration of sin replaces the confession of sin, God removes His presence. Singing "God Bless America" doesn't bring Him back.

W E'RE CHANGING THIS NATION from the inside out, and we plan on getting a key to *this* city too. And for those right-wing bigots who think they can stop us, we're already in their "living rooms every night on prime-time TV—they're laughing at our humor."[1]

We heard these words from the stage at a Human Rights Campaign (HRC) dinner in Charlotte, North Carolina. Over a thousand activists from across our state gathered at the Charlotte Convention Center to celebrate, and further orchestrate, the takeover of traditional America with an emphasis now in our very own city.

It was a hot summer night outside, and the spiritual heat in the room kept rising as the evening wore on. We wanted to know the HRC's plans for Charlotte. But we had heard enough and finally left. Yes, we had bought tickets to attend this event. We thought it was important for us to hear firsthand what they had to say and what the group's plan was for our city and nation.

In the last ten years we have seen this organization's determination to deliver on its words, culminating with a redefinition of marriage by the Supreme Court in the summer of 2015. The very institution that has upheld civil society has been redefined right before our eyes. In early 2015, we watched in dismay as the Charlotte City Council narrowly defeated a transgender bathroom bill—written by the HRC—that would have declared *all* restrooms and locker rooms in *any* public place open to "self-identifying" males or females. After this initial defeat, the bill was later passed in early 2016.

Seriously? In our city? In America? None of this seems right . . . because it's *not* right.

Back in 2004, we attended a gay pride event at Marshall Park in uptown Charlotte. We believed this would be a strategic time to *be* the church in our city and share the love of Jesus with many who were trying to find the love of a father in the arms of another man (or woman). We'll never forget what we witnessed that day. We saw thousands of people swarming around festival booths with some of the most lewd images you could ever imagine and having conversations that would turn your stomach sour. Our hearts broke for the individuals trapped in this lifestyle. Our message was simple: "God has a better way."

As the day progressed, so did the festivities. A tall man, dressed as a woman, danced for the growing crowd, and a ten-year-old boy walked up with a dollar bill and tucked it into the man's underwear. The crowd went crazy. A female comedian then took the main stage and opened up her act with jokes about young children becoming gay.

Just writing about these events breaks our hearts all over again. Our friend Dr. Michael Brown helped us put words to our thoughts and feelings, telling us, "Boys, we need to *reach out to the people* with compassion, yet *resist* the agenda with courage."[2]

The doctor is right.

 Today we must reach out and resist. Reach out with compassion to people trapped in sin, but resist with courage the agenda to impose that sin.

What we witnessed that day in our own city was simply a by-product of our nation's rejection of God and methodical removal of His standards from our lives. Today, as this chapter's opening verse states, we are doing what is "right in [our] own eyes," not God's. Consider Proverbs 21:2:

> Every man's way is right in his own eyes,
> But the LORD weighs the hearts.

WORLD TURNED UPSIDE DOWN

There is no doubt we are witnessing the systematic redefinition of biblical values and the elimination of Christian influence from our culture. Religious convictions, especially on the subjects of marriage and life, are touted as the new sins of modern America.

And standing on those convictions will cost you something; ever increasingly, this means *inside* the church as well.

Imagine if all the airline pilots decided they no longer needed the guidance of control towers and air traffic controllers. They declare that the entire system we have used to fly safely for decades is now unnecessary and outdated. The pilots decide they want to go their own way, choose for themselves, and chart their own course. Tragic crashes would take place all over the country. While the pilots might have fun for a while, lives would be devastated as a result, and soon flying would be rendered dangerous and useless. The desire for individual freedom from structure would destroy our ability to fly. Who would want to risk their lives in a completely unaccountable sky?

God is the One who enabled America to become great. His Word has been our "control tower," inspiring our founding principles and navigating our historical flight pattern. But now we consider His rules unnecessary and outdated. We want to fly where we want, when we want, in a completely unaccountable sky. We have progressively forgotten the unseen hand that has lifted us to great heights as a nation. We have grown weary of His moral constraints and repulsed by His sovereign rule. So we cut off the radio to the tower and ignore the flight instructions. In essence, we've become our own gods, doing what is right in our own eyes.

A quick glimpse at history reveals how we have steadily shut off all communication with the tower. Just to name a few:

1962, *Engel v. Vitale*: prayer removed from school[3]
1963, *Abington School District v. Schempp*: Bible reading
    expelled from school[4]
1973, *Roe v. Wade*: abortion legalized[5]

1980, *Stone v. Graham*: posting of Ten Commandments removed from schools[6]

1992, *Casey v. Planned Parenthood*: humans, not God, define life[7]

2015, *Obergefell v. Hodges*: marriage redefined[8]

What God calls depraved, our culture now calls diversity. What God calls blessed, our culture calls bigoted. The words of the prophets are stinging us again with an eerie, modern relevance:

> Woe to those who call evil good, and good evil;
> Who substitute darkness for light and light for darkness.
>
> —ISAIAH 5:20

 The same rising tide of evil that makes cowards run makes champions rise.

In 2015, Dr. James Dobson wrote, "I do not recall a time when the institutions of marriage and the family have faced such peril, or when the forces arrayed against them were more formidable or determined."[9] When asked what the final years of the twentieth century looked like for the church in America, Dr. Elton Trueblood, born in 1900 and former chaplain for Harvard and Stanford universities, responded, "By the year 2000, Christians will be a conscious minority surrounded by an arrogant militant paganism."[10]

What prophetic words! But while these seem to be coming true in our day, this is certainly no time to shrink back in defeat. Precisely when the stakes are high and the game is on the line is when champions play their best. That time is now. We need overcomers like Daniel to arise once again in our nation—people of a different spirit, gripped by an eternal perspective, and willing to live with conviction, commitment, and courage—whatever the cost.

Leonard Ravenhill commented on Trueblood's prophetic words:

> The early church was walled in on one side with the mightiest military machine in history, the power of Rome. It was walled in on the other side with Greek intellectualism. It was blocked ahead by the monopoly the Jews thought they had on God. Those men who turned the world upside down had no colossal intellectual capacity. No great financial backing. No social standing. They were about the most despised men in and around Jerusalem. And yet they broke out somehow—and later it was said that they turned the world upside-down.[11]

MERCY ON AMERICA

"But if the people of that nation stop doing the evil they have done, I will change my mind and not carry out my plans to bring disaster to them."

—JEREMIAH 18:8 NCV

God longs to have mercy on America. He is filled with compassion and kindness, wanting us to turn back to Him. But we have to confess we have rejected God, and until then, He will not pour out His mercy on us (2 Chronicles 7:14).

God's love is unconditional, but God's mercy is conditioned upon our repentance.

Our actions have left us to the wiles of the Enemy, the one who seeks to "rob, kill, and destroy" (John 10:10 CEV). To be clear, our current cultural crises are not the *cause* of God's judgment; they are the *results*. We rejected God and His ways; therefore, we are now experiencing the fruits of that decision, and we pray just as Daniel did: "Lord, you are righteous, but this day we are covered with shame—the people of Judah and the inhabitants of Jerusalem and all Israel" (Daniel 9:7 NIV).

We often refer to the Holy Spirit's fruit (Galatians 5:22–23), and we should. But we must be mindful that the flesh also produces bad fruit if we cultivate its lifestyle. Paul warned us of this.

> Now the deeds of the flesh are evident, which are: immorality, impurity, sensuality, idolatry, sorcery, enmities, strife, jealousy, outbursts of anger, disputes, dissensions, factions, envying, drunkenness, carousing, and things like these, of which I forewarn you, just as I have forewarned you, that those who practice such things will not inherit the kingdom of God.
> —GALATIANS 5:19–21

THE PRESSURE'S ON

As we stated in our introduction, Christians in America today are experiencing pressure, not persecution. But real persecution is happening around the world as believers refuse to bow the knee to anything but Jesus. Thank God for their boldness! We must follow their lead.

Donald Knoblet is a friend of ours who serves in Shenyang, China. He told us, "The Christians here have no fear of the lions in the coliseum. Honestly, they make me nervous with their boldness. They have no fear of traveling into places like North Korea and Pakistan to share the gospel!"[12] For Chinese Christians the freedom of religion doesn't even exist. But the world is witnessing their faithfulness and boldness as the church in China is exploding! We pray the same would happen in America.

Yet the pressure we're experiencing may indeed become persecution. As David Platt said in his book *Counter Culture*, "The cost of biblical conviction in contemporary culture is growing steeper every day, and we are not far removed from sharing more soberly in the sufferings of Christ."[13] Sharing in these sufferings will happen in America if we don't turn back to God. What's vital for the church today is not to figure out how to deal with persecution, but how to get right with God—and to lead our nation back to Him.

 If persecution comes to America, perseverance in Christ will reinvigorate believers and reinforce the body of Christ.

The answer to our crisis is quite simple: repentance. Listen to Daniel's prayer for his nation in Babylon, a powerful example of how we should pray today:

> To the Lord our God belong compassion and forgiveness, for we have rebelled against Him; nor have we obeyed the voice of the Lord our God, to walk in His teachings which He set

before us through His servants the prophets. . . . As it is written in the law of Moses, all this calamity has come on us; yet
we have not sought the favor of the LORD our God by turning
from our iniquity and giving attention to Your truth. . . . O
Lord, hear! O Lord, forgive! O Lord, listen and take action!
For Your own sake, O my God, do not delay, because Your
city and Your people are called by Your name.

—DANIEL 9:9–19

A TRANSFORMING QUESTION

Years ago we had the privilege of meeting with Dr. Erwin Lutzer,
pastor of the historic Moody Church in Chicago. We asked if
he thought God was going to judge America. His answer sent
us on a journey that helped pave the way and set the tone for
this book. Dr. Lutzer said, "Guys, the question is not, 'Will God
judge America?' The question is, 'What does faithfulness look
like in the midst of God's judgment?'"[14]

Living Among Lions is our attempt to answer that question.
We believe Daniel's model of transformation, even while exiled
in a foreign land, is what faithfulness should look like in the
midst of God's judgment. For Daniel, these were not occasions
to blend in or backslide, but to persevere. He did not conform;
he *transformed*—and made a difference in Babylon. Transformed
people have the power to transform their world, regardless of the
cultural environment.

So let's buckle up and jump back a few thousand years to
visit a young Jewish man named Daniel, who had just arrived in
a pagan country.

AUTHORS' NOTE 2

BABYLON

He ordered him to teach them the literature and language of the Chaldeans.

—Daniel 1:4

 Christians should not blend in, but mix in with the culture—like chocolate chips in a batch of cookie dough.

WE'RE ADDICTED TO CHOCOLATE chip cookie dough. Don't judge us—you probably are too. When we were kids, if we opened our refrigerator and saw a bucket of this heavenly manna, it was gone in no time! It was even better if we saw our mom making chocolate chip cookie dough from scratch. We'd stand right beside her like two thoroughbreds on race day ready to kick the gate open. Sandwiching her little five-foot-two frame, we would watch her take all the ingredients—flour, butter, vanilla, baking soda, salt, eggs, sugar (did we say sugar?), and mix them all together. Once she was done, there was a batch of brown heaven staring at us. Just one more thing was needed—the almighty chocolate chips.

As we watched our mom strike the final chord to her

masterpiece by adding in these sweet little morsels of goodness, we learned a valuable lesson. All the other ingredients actually blended in together, losing their original form, no longer recognizable in the batter. But the chocolate chips never did— they only *mixed in*. In each bite we had no clue what was butter, sugar, or flour, but we always knew when we bit into a chocolate chip. Things only got better as she would pop them into the oven. Even in this fiery baking chamber, the chips still maintained their distinct shape and size. They never lost their "chocolate-chippiness," even when the heat turned up.

Hungry for some yet? (*Jason: I just caught David gnawing on his laptop cover.*) Isn't it awesome when God uses sweet treats to teach us spiritual truths? Christians are to be the chocolate chips in the cookie dough of culture. We are to *mix in*, not *blend in*— we keep our form, remaining completely distinct and separate, even when the heat is turned up. And it's the chocolate chips that make the cookies great.

We can't imagine cookie dough without chocolate chips. Talk about living in captivity!

 Christians are to be the chocolate chips in the cookie dough of culture. We are to *mix in*, not *blend in*—we keep our form, remaining completely distinct and separate—yet we should make the batch great!

The story of Daniel and his three buddies gives us an amazing example of what "mixing in" looks like in real life. Though it would have been easy for them to blend into the batch of pagan culture, they chose to keep their form, stand up, and stand out for their God. Even when they were put into a literal oven, they still maintained their distinction. The story of their lives paints a beautiful picture of what faithfulness looks like in the midst of God's judgment.

MIXING INTO THE MADNESS

Daniel, whose name means "God is my judge," was likely a teenager when he was taken captive to Babylon.[1] The southern kingdom of Judah—like the northern kingdom of Israel before it—had sinned against God and fallen under His judgment. After years of continued rebellion, even though God had sent prophets to warn them and encourage their repentance, the people continued in their depravity. So God raised up an enemy to defeat them and remove them from the Land of Promise (Daniel 1:1–2).

The king of Babylon took many Jews into exile, choosing the "best of the best" to train and then serve in his court. Four of them were young men named Daniel (renamed Belteshazzar) and his three friends—Hananiah (Shadrach), Mishael (Meshach), and Azariah (Abed-nego). They were from the royal bloodline and had mad-crazy wisdom and skills. They were the millennial rock stars of their day.

Upon arriving in Babylon, they were taken into the king's court for three years to be indoctrinated into their new culture. They would be served the finest food and wine available. Every day would be an all-you-can-eat buffet from the best five-star chefs in the region. Daniel and his buddies lived in the lap of luxury, treated with privilege and surrounded by the brightest and most beautiful people in the Hollywood of their day. Surely the temptation to melt into their new, pagan culture was present on many levels (vv. 3–7).

But right out of the gate, these guys kept their form. (Chocolate chips!) Though they mixed in—learning the nation's history, principles, and language; respecting its government as much as possible; and versing themselves in all things Babylonian—Daniel and his friends still refused to *blend* in. They distinctly remained God's men (vv. 8–17).

This concept of mixing without melting reminds us of a quote most often attributed to Thomas Jefferson but that is really of unknown origin: "In matters of style, swim with the current; in matters of principle, stand like a rock."[2]

And stand like a rock they did—even in a land notorious for sin, sensuality, and self-indulgence. Babylon is referred to more than three hundred times in the Bible and is often used as a symbol for ungodliness, sexual promiscuity, and idolatry.[3] Check out Revelation 18:1–5:

> After these things I saw another angel coming down from heaven, having great authority, and the earth was illumined with his glory. And he cried out with a mighty voice, saying, "Fallen, fallen is Babylon the great! She has become a dwelling place of demons and a prison of every unclean spirit, and a prison of every unclean and hateful bird. For all the nations have drunk of the wine of the passion of her immorality, and the kings of the earth have committed acts of immorality with her, and the merchants of the earth have become rich by the wealth of her sensuality."
>
> I heard another voice from heaven, saying, "Come out of her, my people, so that you will not participate in her sins

and receive of her plagues; for her sins have piled up as high as heaven, and God has remembered her iniquities."

At the time of Daniel's deportation in 605 BC, Babylon was the most powerful empire in the world—the cultural center for art and industry, creating great wealth and luxury for its citizens.[4] This environment, coupled with blatant idolatry and fascination with the occult, created the perfect storm of sin and rebellion among its people.

While conducting research for this book, we googled phrases related to "comparing America to Babylon" and got almost twenty million results![5] Although there are major differences between America and Babylon, there are some alarming similarities: wealth, world influence, natural beauty, sexual promiscuity, increasing paganism, and more. So if Daniel could live faithfully there, we can do it here.

During their three years of training, Daniel and his friends were fully indoctrinated into Babylonian culture, one that did not and would not honor their God. Persecution in those days wasn't a rude tweet or a mean Facebook post but actual, straight-up, cold-blooded execution.

These four young men knew God. They had studied the Law and the prophets and knew the Scriptures well. They were familiar with the psalms, including the passage in which King David wrote,

> I am surrounded by lions;
> I lie down with those who devour men.
> Their teeth are spears and arrows;
> their tongues are sharp swords.
>
> —PSALM 57:4 HCSB

David's God was their God. They were going to live faithfully, just as David did before them, even among lions. While many "lions" roamed in and out of the king's court throughout Daniel's time in Babylon, he and his friends remained distinct, prophetic voices in the midst of this pagan land. Daniel's first test came when King Nebuchadnezzar had a disturbing dream. Believing dreams were often spiritually significant, the king wanted his wise men to give its interpretation. But first, he demanded they tell him the dream itself—without his help! When the wise men confessed they couldn't possibly do it, the king decided to kill them all. (*Jason: I bet David would've started sucking his thumb again!*)

Can you imagine how impossible and unfair this must have seemed? But as God's men have always done throughout history, Daniel and his friends dropped to their knees in prayer and then stepped up to the plate—even in the face of death—to deliver God's message. They sought their God for the king's answer even while encircled by "lions" threatening their lives. And God answered. God gave Daniel a correct interpretation of Nebuchadnezzar's dream, and the king's wrath cooled. God not only preserved the lives of these four faithful men but also rescued *all* of Babylon's wise men from certain death. And that was only the beginning. God's ultimate plan was to use this scenario to drive a stake of testimony deep into the ground of Babylon's royalty.

When Daniel delivered his message in the name of his God, the world's most powerful man fell on his face and gave glory to Him. "The king said to Daniel, 'Your God is indeed God of gods, Lord of kings, and a revealer of mysteries, since you were able to reveal this mystery'" (Daniel 2:47 HCSB). The king encountered Daniel's God that day because he had encountered God's man.

Because Daniel himself was transformed, he was able to transform his world!

The king promoted Daniel, and he then brought his three friends up with him.

 Trusting God's promises and following God's practices will bring God's promotion.

Daniel's courage was contagious. His buddies had their turn to stand strong in the face of death. A few years after Daniel interpreted Nebuchadnezzar's dream, the king made a golden statue and commanded his kingdom to worship it (Daniel 3). When the music played, the entire crowd bowed low—except for three men: Shadrach, Meshach, and Abed-nego. Daniel's friends all stood straight, knowing the heat was coming if they remained on their feet. But they did remain—and into the furnace they went!

In the same way Christians would refuse to bow to the Roman emperor centuries later, Shadrach, Meshach, and Abed-nego refused to bow the knee to the Babylonian king. And even the fiery furnace could not destroy them. The king looked into the raging fire—flames that had just destroyed some of his own men—and saw Daniel's three friends walking around, unharmed, and joined by a fourth man who "is like a son of the gods!" (v. 25).

When the king called the men out, he found them unaffected by the fire—their hair was not singed, their clothing was not damaged, and they didn't even smell like smoke! As a result, the great king who had exalted his own image against God now publicly confessed that there was no other god like the God of these Jews. The king even made it illegal for anyone in his kingdom to speak against the God of Shadrach, Meshach, and Abed-nego (vv. 26–29).

But this moment of humility didn't go deep enough into Nebuchadnezzar's heart. His prideful disposition rose again to defy God's sovereignty over the kingdom of Babylon. So again God tapped Daniel on the shoulder to give testimony to His kingdom on earth (Daniel 4). This time Daniel had to bring a message of judgment against Nebuchadnezzar, telling what would happen if he did not repent of his arrogance and wickedness (vv. 19–24).

 God has called us to be His faithful messengers even if His message is not popular.

Even after a clear warning from the Lord, Nebuchadnezzar boasted in the glory of his kingdom as if he had achieved it all himself. The king declared that he built his own kingdom with his own strength. But in a dream, God reminded Him, "the Most High is ruler over the realm of mankind and bestows it on whomever He wishes" (v. 25).

Nebuchadnezzar refused to humble himself, so God removed his ability to reason. The king literally became like an animal. His hair grew like eagle feathers and his fingernails like eagle claws. He lived like a beast away from other humans (v. 33). He must have been quite a sight. (*David: I've seen Jason look like this a time or two.*) According to Daniel's interpretation of the king's dream, this condition would last seven years. He promised Nebuchadnezzar, after that period, "your kingdom will be assured to you after you recognize that it is Heaven that rules" (v. 26).

When the seven years ended and the king's reason returned, he humbled himself and praised the Most High God. He honored the One "who lives forever; for His dominion is an ever-lasting dominion . . . for all His works are true and His ways just, and He is able to humble those who walk in pride" (vv. 34–37). As a result of his humble repentance, the king was reestablished in his kingdom.

Throughout these stories, we see Daniel and his friends living with conviction, commitment, and courage—even in the face of death. Whether they saw God with their physical eyes or not, they knew He was right there with them in Spirit, every step of the way. Because they were faithful to God in Babylon, He made them thrive there. Because they allowed God to transform them, they were able to transform their world.

GOING ALL IN

There's an old Cherokee legend often shared and written about that describes the rite of passage of how boys became men. The father took his son to the forest, blindfolded him, and left him sitting on a tree stump. The boy was required to sit there the whole night, not removing the blindfold until he saw the rays of the morning sun shine through. He was not to cry out for help to anyone.

Once he survived the night, he was considered a man by the tribe. He could not tell anyone of the experience because each boy had to come into manhood on his own. Throughout the night, with no weapon, he could hear the noises of the forest all around him. But he had to sit unmoving, never touching the blindfold.

Finally, after a long night, the sun appeared, and he removed his blindfold. In that moment he then discovered his dad had been sitting nearby all along. The father had been at watch the entire time, protecting his son.[6]

Likewise, Daniel was never alone—and neither are we. The God who hung the moon and stars, who made the land and sea, is the living God and our loving Father. He is with us, encouraging us to be like Daniel and empowering us to be like Jesus. "Be strong and courageous, do not be afraid or tremble at them, for the LORD your God is the one who goes with you. He will not fail you or forsake you" (Deuteronomy 31:6).

Daniel's story is certainly not just some cool Bible tale about courage and bravery but a very real legacy giving us hope and inspiring us to live the same way today. It's *our* story as well— *our* heritage. For all who choose to go all in for God, the book of Daniel is written. We can live among lions because God is with us, watching over us to protect us. All we have to do is stand. And if we go down, we go down standing up, knowing He's right here with us every step of the way.

Daniel's life forever marked Babylon, and we can do the same in our world. God has transformed us, so we can transform the world.

The best part of this entire story is that the same One who walked in the furnace with Shadrach, Meshach, and Abed-nego still walks with us today. The same Spirit that shut the mouths of the beasts for Daniel in the lions' den is here for us, empowering us to live faithfully among the lions of our day.

This is *our* time. *Our* story.

This is *your* time. *Your* story.

Let it begin!

PART I

CONVICTION THAT TRANSFORMS MY HEART

W E HAVE BUILT OUR companies on five core principles, discussed in detail in *Whatever the Cost*. One of those principles is "Be a Fountain, Not a Drain."

Think about a water fountain. When you are thirsty and press the button, what comes out? Water—nourishment for your body. For a fountain to give nourishment, it has to be plugged into a source. If not, you can press the button all day, but nothing will come out. There's nothing inside the fountain to satisfy your thirst.

Likewise, if we do not connect to God as our Life Source, when our "button is pressed," nothing comes out to nourish others (John 15:4–5). But when we do connect, divine life will flow through us. Transformation begins with us. This is why this book's first section deals with conviction. We must develop the inner person before we develop outer disciplines and before we try to change the world. Otherwise, our disciplines become religious burdens and we become a horde of noisy radicals with lots of ideas and no real substance. But when we connect to Christ and live from the inside out, disciplines become our joy, and changing our world becomes natural.

God always works from the inside out—from the heart of man to the heart of culture. So as we develop our internal life in Christ, we will also develop the spiritual resources to live with dignity and act with power when the lions of our culture roar against us.

As you read this first section on conviction, reflect on what's inside you. The rest of the book hinges on the transformation of your heart. So take your time and be honest. Allow the Holy Spirit to probe and do His work on the inside. You'll be glad you did.

The conviction that transforms your heart comes when you . . .

Know God
Know Your Identity
Think Your Identity
Build Your Worldview
Choose Reverence

CHAPTER 1

KNOW GOD

This is eternal life, that they may know You, the only true God, and Jesus Christ whom You have sent.

—JOHN 17:3

 Know Jesus, know courage. If you want to be courageous, you have to first know the Courageous One.

GOD GIVES US THE opportunity to become catalysts for bringing transformation to the world, but His offer comes with a choice. We can sit on the sidelines and watch, or we can get in the game, allowing Him to bring His transformational power to the world around us.

This transformation begins on the inside of us, and personal transformation always begins with a genuine, intimate relationship with God Himself. Nothing we do in this world will matter if we don't get this part right. So we begin with knowing God personally.

When we cultivate a heart-to-heart friendship with God, He changes us into powerful people who then have the resources to change our world.

> And He said to them, "Follow Me, and I will make you fishers of men."
>
> —MATTHEW 4:19

Daniel's power to transform his world came from the outflow of his relationship with God. But his surrender to God was not an eleventh-hour Hail Mary on the road to Babylon; instead, it was an intentional decision to be in an intimate relationship with Him—to *know* God—many years before the captivity and deportation of his country. A relationship this strong is not built overnight in the face of a crisis.

Prior to his time in Babylon, all we know about Daniel was that he came from the royal family and was a young stud—handsome, intelligent, wise, discerning, and knowledgeable. (*David: I sense Jason's jealousy as we write this.*) Yet the fruit of his life—even at such a young age—made this one thing abundantly clear: Daniel knew his God.

So when the crisis came down, Daniel rose above it. Even amid judgment and captivity, his conviction matched God's call to flourish in Babylon.

 When our level of conviction matches God's call, courage can crush any crisis.

Daniel's faith was his own, not just relegated to Sunday morning church attendance or belonging to the "right" denomination.

His faith was deeply personal. The Lord was *his* God. Check out the wording of the first commandment, quoted by Jesus in Matthew 22:37: "You shall love the Lord *your* God with all *your* heart, and with all *your* soul, and with all *your* mind." Interesting that Jesus didn't just say, "love God," but rather "love . . . *your* God." The greatest commandment is to love God as your own—to know Him personally and intimately—so you may say, regardless of what others choose, "I will serve the Lord."

But before you can know God in a deeply personal way, you have to meet Him. Fortunately for us, like Daniel, that day came at a young age.

A WHOLE NEW BALL GAME

The Christian school we attended in Garland, Texas, was part of an Independent Baptist church. The pastor and staff wore full suits, and the music minister parted his hair from one ear to the other. Red carpet, wooden pews, and old hymnals . . . yeah, the whole nine yards. We were always afraid of getting cornered by the youth pastor who'd ask us to go door-to-door visiting on a Saturday afternoon.

At Garland Christian Academy, we gave our hearts to Jesus. We didn't know what this decision fully meant at the time—and there was a part of us that was more interested in "fire insurance" than knowing the Father—but we came to learn that God was the very thing our little hearts were searching for. This was the beginning of a relationship between the Creator and two of His human creations.

When I (Jason) was about sixteen years old, my relationship

with the Lord kicked into another gear. One morning I woke up early and went outside to read my Bible and hit a quick workout before school. The air was crisp, and it was well before dawn. After reading, I lay down on the workout bench to do some lifting. Right away, I felt a gentle wind pick up that turned my attention away from exercise. I looked to the sky and saw the clouds rolling by. I just lay there, completely still and quiet. The sky looked enormous, filled with stars beaming down at me. Thoughts of God flooded my mind, and I tuned in to Him as the Creator. I was deeply impressed by what I saw—and realized. This was the first time I can remember sitting back and simply admiring God's massive handiwork.

But this thought became the gamechanger: *The same God who created all of this knows me and loves me.*

This was a defining moment—a watershed in the budding spiritual life of a teenage boy. I clearly remember that feeling of wanting to know and love God in return. I had already loved Him enough to give Him my heart. But now I got the sense that I really didn't *know* Him as deeply as I could—or should. I had experienced conviction of my sin, but I had not yet learned to live with conviction in an intimate relationship with God.

I knew I was His, but now I wanted Him to be *mine.*

The next three years, before David and I left home for Liberty University, proved to be a time of explosive growth in the Lord for us both. By the time we were college freshmen, we could say we truly knew the Lord. Like Daniel's, our faith was now our own and deeply personal.

After four years at Liberty, we entered the world of professional baseball. For the first time in our lives, we were in a totally foreign environment. People in our new world not only lacked interest in the things of God but also often mocked them. The friendly confines of our comfortable Christian environment had been replaced by a strange land. And our relationship with the Lord was put to the test.

We did the only thing we knew to do: stay faithful to God by drawing strength from our growing relationship with Him. We knew God, and He knew us. So we understood our role in this new environment and were able to remain secure in that identity. We didn't carry index cards around the clubhouse with how-to lists or reminders to say no to temptation and shine the light of Jesus. Instead, we simply focused on our relationship with Him. So even in a foreign situation often opposed to our faith, we kept up our pursuit to know God better. And the more we got to know Him, the more of Him we wanted to discover.

As we kept our focus simple and steady, we discovered that the very strain that could have weakened our resolve actually strengthened us. God used this to grow us, because we *knew* Him.

We realized that we were meant to grow through resistance. Strain breaks muscles down so they will grow. The same is true with our souls. God will use the world's resistance to our faith to strengthen us.

 We grow much more through battling our burdens than banking our blessings.

Daniel had to feel something very similar in his exile. Not only did God's people have to endure a level of persecution by leaving their homeland for Babylon, but they also had to face the tempting allure of its godless pleasures. The Jews lived there for seventy years before getting the chance to return home. Many were born and raised in that pagan environment. During that time, some probably strayed from their faith and embraced the culture, while others stood strong and resisted.

So what carried Daniel and his friends through this moral maze, causing them to stand strong from beginning to end? *They knew their God.* They were His, and He was theirs. Their faithful lives and powerful exploits in Babylon were birthed out of their intimate knowledge of Him.

THIS IS PERSONAL

We're no theologians by any stretch, but we have discovered a simple truth: you can know about God in your head, *intellectually*, but not know Him in your heart, *intimately*. Intimate knowledge of God is what creates conviction—the type that will stand even in the face of lions.

When we take a stand for the Lord, we don't do it because we know all the stories in the Bible and can quote the Roman Road verses verbatim. Although we have an intellectual knowledge of the Scripture, we also have the courage of conviction because we have an intimate relationship with Jesus. We enjoy a firm resolve to remain faithful to Him because we love Him. Through this intimacy we also have experiences time and again when we see God move in power. Intimacy, coupled with experience, brings deeper commitment.

The more we came to know God intimately, the more we desired to understand Him intellectually. And the more we understood Him intellectually, the deeper we grew with Him intimately.

God illustrates this concept beautifully in the covenant of marriage. In fact, that is one of the reasons why we believe this institution is under attack today. Physical intimacy between a husband and wife is the outward manifestation of a much deeper spiritual truth: the covenant bond—the intimate knowledge—shared by Christ and His church (Ephesians 5:22–33). Our definition of intimacy is "to be fully known and fully accepted." In marriage, both partners reveal themselves completely to their spouses, and each spouse fully accepts the other unconditionally. The physical union between the two is a picture of this knowing—a two-way street of knowledge leading to intimacy and oneness.

For example, Matthew 1:25 says, Joseph did not "know" Mary until after Jesus was born (HCSB). They were not physically intimate prior to His birth. But clearly they did know each other in another sense—intellectually; they just did not yet know each other experientially. This distinction illustrates a spiritual truth. We can know God theoretically but not know Him experientially—on the level of intimacy, which creates *conviction* in our hearts. Notice what Jesus says to those who will stand before Him and claim their good works as keys to entering His kingdom: "I never *knew* you; depart from Me" (Matthew 7:23). These people, though they had an intellectual knowledge of God evidenced by good works, did not have an intimate knowledge of Him through total surrender.

Surrender was the way Daniel and his friends knew God. They carried that relationship from Jerusalem to the height of Babylon—then through the furnace, into the lions' den, and back to the top of the kingdom—all while remaining faithful to God. They *knew* Him, and all of their actions revealed that intimate knowledge of Him.

CONVICTION THAT TRANSFORMS MY HEART

BECOMING AN ACTION HERO

Those who know God intimately will live faithfully when evil manifests itself. God showed this to Daniel in a vision: "By smooth words he will turn to godlessness those who act wickedly toward the covenant, but the people who know their God will display strength and take action" (Daniel 11:32). This verse, widely believed to be prophecy from Daniel, also describes what kind of people will flourish during that time of persecution: those, just like Daniel, who know their God and take action when the heat is turned up. They display supernatural strength, doing God's work on the earth.

That one little verse, buried in the midst of a chapter of prophecy, shows the key to how God's kingdom breaks into our world: through people of faith who thrive in the midst of godlessness. What's their secret? They *know* their God.

True love doesn't manifest itself merely in our words, but also in our deeds. How do those you love know you love them? Is it only because you tell them? No, it's because you show them. Love must be seen and experienced.

Let's look at this concept a little deeper. When evil rises up, those who know their God will do two very recognizable things.

1. Display Strength

Here are some qualities of visible spiritual strength:

+ Resolve. People of resolve live with conviction, secure in firm decisions that are based on a proven biblical standard. This enables them to take a consistent stand against the pressures of persecution and temptation. People with this kind of inner strength *petition God* for boldness rather than *position themselves* for security. Why? Because they know the source of strength is not in them, but in God. The standard by which they live is based not on their own opinions or anyone else's, but on God.

+ Readiness. People who live in readiness won't give in to fear but will press through it even in the face of death. The things that make most people flee the scene will cause these folks to run to the roar! Why? Their disciplined conviction has stored up the courage to be ready for the crisis. You cannot call on a reserve that is not available.

 Readiness is realized before the roar is heard.

+ Resolution. For those who know God, His Word is not "flexible" when it comes to absolutes—but solid and unyielding, grounded in firm and faithful determination. They know and teach that truth transforms people. You don't change truth. Truth changes you.

Those who *know* their God will be people of resolve, will live in readiness, and will be resolute in their beliefs and actions.

2. Take Action

Those who know their God will not be afraid to take action in the face of a dark culture. Here are a few words that describe these action-takers:

- Proactive. Simply grieving over a darkened culture is not enough. Complaining and criticizing won't change a thing. Those who know God must do something—take action. They are proactive about knowing their God and living a kingdom-centered life. They're God's agents in both the work of evangelism and in being salt and light in the culture. As we move forward, we will share plenty of practical ways to be proactive as Christians.

- Principled. Those who know God intimately and intellectually have an arsenal of truths to create an offense and defense for any situation. They have principles in place through daily discipline to read God's Word that help them make their choice prior to having to make the decision. Like Daniel and his friends, the decision is easy—"We're standing by our convictions!"

- Passionate. We won't press on if we don't fully believe in the reason why we must stand. Our passion for God is built in and through an intimate relationship with Him. You don't work through problems in a marriage when you aren't passionate about loving your spouse. You won't stand in the face of pressure or persecution unless you are passionate about the One you are living for. Whatever the cost, a heart of conviction will also be filled with passion.

Those who engage God by displaying strength and taking action will engage their culture—in exactly that order. Engage God, and then engage the culture.

FIRST THINGS FIRST

These questions are worth asking, and answering, with honesty: Do you know God? Are you displaying courage and strength or fear and weakness? Is your life characterized by kingdom activity or by lethargy and passivity?

If you do not know God, now is the time to start. Begin your journey by seeking Him through an intimate relationship with Jesus. Put this book down, and do business with God right where you are, right now. God says, "You will seek Me and find Me when you search for Me with all your heart" (Jeremiah 29:13). Do not focus on becoming strong or taking action. Focus on *Him*, knowing *Him* and pursuing *Him*. Then strength and action will follow through the relationship.

How do you begin? Bible teachers and counselors often define *intimacy* with the phrase "into me, see." While this is certainly a great principle for marriage and other close relationships, it is also vitally important for our relationship with God.

God already sees into us and knows us intimately: "O LORD, You have searched me and known me" (Psalm 139:1). So now our part is to open ourselves up to Him—to share our deepest desires, struggles, doubts, burdens, and victories. Our hearts' goal is to hide nothing from the God who knows us—to bear our hearts to the lover of our souls. The fruit of Daniel's life makes clear that he had this kind of friendship with God. To live a Daniel-life, we must be intimate with God. The constant prayer of our hearts should be "Father, 'into me, see.' I hide nothing from you."

MAJOR MINOR MINISTRY

When I (Jason) was with the Baltimore Orioles in the minor leagues, I soon became known as "the Christian dude from Texas." That wasn't my goal at all. I was just living the best I knew how among the guys. But as my reputation as a Christian grew, so did my concern for the souls of the men on my team. The guys became more than "projects" for my Christian witness; I saw them as people God loved and cared for. They weren't just ball players but people created and loved by God.

One of them was a pitcher who had also played college basketball. He was tall and lanky with a cannon for an arm. (David couldn't touch his fastball.) This guy was the life of the clubhouse. He always had the TV tuned to some music video channel, laughing and playing around all the time. The ladies loved him—and he knew it. His locker was filled with pictures of women—some dressed and some not so much.

A habitual shower-taker who loved smelling good in between batting practice and game time, this teammate would shower up and then spray cologne all over his body. While we were on the field stretching, we could smell him the moment he stepped out of the clubhouse. He seemed to relish his reputation as he rolled onto the field with a big smile and an even bigger swagger in his step.

We struck up a fast friendship even though our lives were vastly different. My goal wasn't to change him—or any of the other guys for that matter. I just wanted to be a light in the middle of pumping music and pornographic pictures. God would do the changing of hearts, not me. Knowing God gave me the strength I needed to stand strong. The guys were watching me—especially this particular player—to see if my faith was genuine or just a label.

The night I was released from the team, I was sitting at my locker with my head in my hands when I felt a tap on my shoulder. Fighting back the tears, I looked up, and there was my pitcher friend. He pulled me up and hugged me as tight as he could. Then he reached out and handed me a gift that he said was especially for me. I looked, and there was his trademark bottle of cologne.

I could tell he was having a hard time processing my release. It flew in the face of his traditional thinking that "bad things shouldn't happen to good people." With all seriousness, he looked right at me and said, "You're the real deal, man. I love you and don't want you to ever forget me. When you smell my cologne, think of me, and pray for me."

That night my dream of playing in the big leagues died right there at my locker. But God used this situation to teach me that He isn't concerned with fame by the world's standards. He is concerned with *faithfulness* by *His* standards. My role in professional baseball was not to make it out under the big lights. My role was to know God and be His man in the clubhouse.

 Never focus on fame by the world's standards but on faithfulness by God's standards. This is where heavenly success will always be found.

The culture of professional baseball was as dark as any I've ever experienced. Being faithful to God is not about being in the *right* environment but knowing God in the midst of *any* environment. My teammate didn't need me to change him. He needed me simply to know God and be faithful to God right where He put me.

Fifteen years later I stumbled onto a box with some of my old baseball stuff. Inside was that little bottle of cologne. The moment I smelled it, my mind rushed back to that clubhouse where I spent the better part of three years trying to live faithfully for God in the midst of the darkness. Just as my pitcher friend had said, that smell did remind me of him—how for a few summers, many years ago, we became true friends who valued each other. Yet I never had to compromise my walk with Jesus to genuinely care for a guy who was the polar opposite of me. I know that just as I'll always remember him, he will always remember me. God used me to plant seeds in him that other faithful souls can now water and, hopefully, one day bring to harvest.

This is no small matter—God gave me strength to remain faithful to Him and be a light in that clubhouse. As a result, I was able to take action in the midst of a dark culture. I know there are other people out there, just like my teammate in the minor leagues, who are longing for men and women who know God to stand up and show them a better way—God's way.

David and I were able to minister to many guys like my buddy because by the time we set foot in any team's clubhouse, we had cultivated a relationship with God that kept us anchored even in the middle of the world's mockery and temptations. The same was true for Daniel in Babylon. He knew his God, so he was strong and able to *act* like God's man in a foreign place. He did not blend in; he mixed in. He did not conform; he transformed. His influence permeated Babylon because Babylon did not permeate him. Daniel's top priority—no matter what opposition he faced—was his covenant relationship with God.

As Christians in twenty-first-century America, the same

applies to us. If we want the strength to transform our world in Jesus' name, to be faithful among the faithless, we ourselves must be transformed—first and foremost—by knowing our God personally and intimately, from the inside out.

CHAPTER 2

KNOW YOUR IDENTITY

The Spirit Himself testifies with our spirit that we are
children of God.

—ROMANS 8:16

 Both God and Satan want to strip you of your
identity—but God wants to replace it with Himself
while Satan just wants to leave you empty.

"I'm a woman trapped in a man's body."
"Why should he be forced to go into the men's room if he
   now self-identifies as a female?"
"We'll allow our children to choose their own gender."

STATEMENTS LIKE THESE ARE becoming more frequent today.
As of this writing, there are fifty-eight different gender
identities available to choose on Facebook, all of which aim to
describe what people *feel* they truly are.[1]

When one of my (Jason's) daughters was three years old, she went through a phase where she told everyone she was a horse. Through her imagination, she felt she was. But as much as she ran around the yard pretending to be a horse, making noises like a horse, and announcing to the neighborhood she was a horse, did anyone, for even a second, believe she was? Of course not. Although for a few days we had to call her by her horse name, Aztec, she eventually forgot about horses and moved on to something else, as all three-year-olds do. We don't concern ourselves with this concept when someone is three, but what about thirteen or thirty-three or even fifty-three?

Unfortunately, many adults are still going through phases and giving in to real-life insecurities, deciding they are something they were never intended to be—or even something they are actively pretending to be. Needless to say, our culture today has an identity crisis. That's the bad news. The good news is, Jesus is in the business of restoring our true identities in Him.

 If we want to know who we are, we need a reference point outside of ourselves. This is where Christianity has the answer. How do we know who we are? Our Creator tells us.

Intimacy with God transforms us into the image of God. No more identity crisis. That is how we—like Daniel—can change our world. We increasingly become *like* the One with whom we have covenant relationship (2 Corinthians 3:18). This is another reason we must know God: we must know who we are *in* God. True Christians must see their identity in Christ alone:

> Do you not know that you are a temple of God and that the Spirit of God dwells in you?
>
> —1 Corinthians 3:16

> And put on the new self, which in the *likeness of* God has been created in righteousness and holiness of the truth.
>
> —Ephesians 4:24

Scripture clearly declares who we are—His loved creation for whom He died (Matthew 8:17)—and describes who we are as followers of Jesus Christ: we are God's children, fellow heirs of His eternal kingdom (Ephesians 3:6). But as our culture rapidly changes around us, Christians in America seem to be suffering from an identity crisis too. Many don't seem to understand the nature of their own transformation when the Holy Spirit came to live inside of them. It's sort of like a spiritual amnesia, causing them to forget who they are and whose they are.

Yet of all people, those who follow God must possess a clear awareness of their identity. Without this, we cannot stand with conviction against the spirit of this age, the way Daniel did. Our identity comes first from knowing who *God* is, then from knowing who *we* are in relation to Him. Without a deep, compelling sense of our true identity, it's impossible to live faithfully in the midst of a darkening culture.

Daniel's defining characteristic was his knowledge of God.

But he also knew his identity in relation to God. This dual knowledge unlocked and empowered his destiny.

MEERKATS AND MONKEY BUSINESS

The Lion King is one of our favorite family movies. (Because we have nine kids between us, our favorite movies are mostly cartoons.) Every time we watch this classic film, we're moved to the core because of its clear message about identity. (*Jason: When we first saw it, I think David scream-cried in the back of the theater.*)

The lion king was the leader of his vast domain. Under his authority, life was good for all the animals. During his reign, the kingdom shined brightly and prospered; there was plenty of food, water, and lush, green landscape as far as the eye could see.

As with all kingdoms, the son was in line to take over leadership one day. But the king's evil brother burned with jealousy, so he arranged for the king to be killed and pinned the blame on the son. The little lion cub panicked when he thought his dad's death was his fault, and he ran far away. With the lion king now dead and the son gone, the evil lion took over the reign of the land. The entire region soon became dark and desolate. A pale shade of gray replaced the kingdom's bright colors.

The son ran until he reached a strange new land where he lived with, surprisingly, a warthog and a meerkat. His new friends trained the young lion to live a carefree life. For the next several years the lion cub lived a simple existence in the jungle, eating plants and bugs provided by his new buddies, blissfully ignorant of his true identity.

But as he grew and became a young adult lion, he began to

struggle with guilt and shame from his past. As he sat outside the forest one evening trying to make sense of the emptiness in his heart, he encountered an odd baboon. After some confusing small talk from the simian stranger, the lion realized the baboon seemed to know more about him than he knew about himself. Finally, in frustration, the lion demanded some answers about how he could possibly know so much about him.

The baboon told him he knew he was the son of a king—and that his father was still alive. Could it be true? His dad, the rightful king of the jungle, was alive this whole time? The monkey then agreed to show the lion where his dad was. Leading him to a stream, he told him to look into the water. The young lion was saddened to see only his reflection, but as he peered into the water again, it began to ripple. Then it happened. As he stared intently, he saw the face of his father in the water. The baboon explained that his dad lived inside of *him*!

For years the young lion had forgotten who he truly was, but in that moment his identity as the king's son was unmistakable. He knew he must return and reclaim the kingdom that was rightfully his.

This classic story clearly illustrates the power of identity. We might feel as if the evil of the world has taken over rule of the land while many of God's children live a carefree lifestyle, blissfully ignorant of their true identity, forgetting who and whose they are. It is time for us, like the young lion, to recover our identity. We are sons and daughters of the Most High King. We must embrace our real identity and roar as lions again.

Sometimes we need a baboon in our lives to remind us of our true identity. While we aren't volunteering to be compared to some smart-aleck monkey (*David: Although Jason looks like one*), we want to remind Christians in this great land that it's time to remember who we are, run to the roar, and return to the life Jesus intended for us to live all along.

LET ME SEE YOUR ID

Even as a teenager, Daniel understood his identity as a child of the one true King. So right out of the gate, when he was offered the Babylonian king's meat and wine, he politely but courageously said, "No, thank you." His actions issued from his God-centered identity. Not even the most powerful leader in the known world offering a buffet of delicacies was going to change that.

Daniel resolved "he would not defile himself" (Daniel 1:8). Traditionally, that meant he would not make himself ceremonially unclean as a Jew by partaking of the foreign king's table (Leviticus 18:30). But, as we will discuss in detail in subsequent chapters, there was more here than meets the eye. Listen to the words of one of our friends and mentors, Old Testament scholar Dr. Michael Brown: "Being forced to live in a foreign country is an inherently defiling experience. In all likelihood, Daniel was simply taking a stand against 'the total program of assimilation,' as other people with conviction have done before and since."[2]

In other words, Daniel was resisting more than food. He was refusing the king's attempt at identity theft. Nebuchadnezzar was trying to absorb Daniel into Babylon's culture through Babylon's delights. Nebuchadnezzar knew that if he could entice Daniel to love Babylon in his heart, then Daniel would permit Babylon to redefine his identity. That is why Daniel saw the king's food and wine as defilement—a corruption he refused.

Daniel didn't need some baboon to remind him of who he was. He had possession of his identity and guarded it with his life—even to the point of eating veggies and water for three years to remain free from Babylon's attempts to violate his personhood. Now *that's* living with conviction.

Remember when Daniel went to the king to interpret his mysterious dream (Daniel 2)? Despite the king's orders to kill all the wise men who couldn't guess its contents, Daniel stepped up to the plate. He bought time to pray and sought answers. He and his friends interceded for their lives with no guarantee God would speak or spare their lives. But they did know who they were—God's men, not the king's men. Therefore, they knew how to respond and take action. They did not run into a corner with their thumbs in their mouths, grieving their coming demise. Nor did they appeal to the king for mercy as did the pagan wise men. Daniel and his friends knew they belonged to heaven's kingdom. And when heaven's citizens are faced with crisis, they pray—they "plead for mercy from the God of heaven" (v. 18 NIV). Whether they lived or died, they would act like men of God by seeking Him for help.

You'll remember that God did answer and miraculously showed Daniel both the dream and its interpretation. If Daniel had lost sight of his identity, he would not have acted as a child of the true King. That loss would have resulted in the deaths of not only Daniel and his friends but also all the wise men in Babylon.

 Knowing our true identity breeds conviction, and conviction fuels our actions.

The king wasted no time when his official ushered Daniel in to interpret the dream. He asked, "Are you able to make known to me the dream which I have seen and its interpretation?" Check out Daniel's response: "As for the mystery about which the king has inquired, neither wise men, conjurers, magicians nor diviners are able to declare it to the king. However, there is a God in heaven who reveals mysteries" (Daniel 2:26–28).

Did you catch that? Daniel had a miracle in his hand—a ticket to glory and promotion in the king's presence. But instead of taking credit for unveiling the mystery, he took the opportunity to give a testimony to the true God of heaven in Babylon's highest court. Because Daniel was secure in his own identity, he could afford to remove himself from the equation and allow God to be promoted. Assurance of who he was enabled him to stick to his real purpose rather than put himself first. Put another way, had he not known the identity God had given him, he would have created his own identity at the expense of others. But Daniel knew this wasn't about increasing his platform or influence for personal gain; it was about keeping his identity as God's man, strategically positioned for His purposes.

 True satisfaction for the Christian is not found in promotion or profit, increase or influence, but in his identity as a child of God.

Look at the results. Daniel saved many lives, gave God supreme testimony amid false gods, and then was promoted as a major player in Babylon's administration. Daniel's identity in his God laid a huge cornerstone in the foundation of his actions. His assurance gave him confidence to refuse the king's delicacies, step up to the plate when his life was on the line, and deny the temptation for personal advancement. That's the power of conviction working out of identity—for all of us.

READING YOUR RÉSUMÉ

Our first interview with the release of our book *Whatever the Cost* took place on *Fox & Friends*. On a freezing February morning in New York, we made our way through icy weather to the Fox studios in Times Square.

After the initial broadcast we were asked to do the *After the Show* for a few more outtakes and another interview. In that interview, the hosts asked us a very interesting question: "When are you guys going to become ministers? You talk so much about God that it just makes sense for you both to become pastors or something."

Our response was simple: "We already are! How you see yourself determines how you conduct yourself, so if you see yourself only as a businessperson, then that's what you'll act like. But if you see yourself as a minister of the gospel first, then that's how you'll act."[3]

They got our point.

As Christians, we *all* are ministers, not because that is our full-time job to make a living but because we know God, love Him, and represent Him wherever we go and in whatever we do. In other words, we are ministers of God's kingdom *because we know who we are in Christ*. Our actions spring from our identity, not our profession—from who we are, not what we do. The church in modern Babylon can no longer afford to leave ministry to the paid experts. The church today needs Daniels from all walks of life who serve God's kingdom simply because they possess an identity as God's saints—God's ministers on a mission (Ephesians 4:11–13).

Daniel was not a member of Jerusalem's professional clergy. He was not a priest. In fact, though he later became a prophet, we have no record of his specific, divine call to prophetic ministry as we see with Isaiah or Jeremiah. Rather, Daniel's calling grew naturally out of his identity as one of God's children—just as ours should. His profession did not matter. Whether a young Jewish noble in Jerusalem, an exile in Babylon, or a pagan king's attendant forced into duty, he acted as a servant and witness of the Most High God because he knew that was his true identity.

Is it time to change the lens through which you view yourself? If you are a faithful follower of Jesus, you are one of God's kids on assignment to bring His kingdom into the world through your influence. If you know God as Daniel did, then you'll also see yourself the way God sees you. And that perspective will enable you to serve Him, no matter the cost.

Daniel's actions flowed from his identity—never the other way around. His reference point for his identity was God—a point outside of himself. This allowed him to fully understand who he was. How he felt and what he did could not add or detract from his identity. Therefore, his actions were consistent throughout his life.

In our society, anytime someone is introduced to another person, the most common first question is, "So what do you do?" The blunt version of this inquiry is actually, "So what do you do to make money?" No one ever asks, "So who are you? Tell me where your heart is. What's your passion?"

We need to be careful not to define ourselves by what we *do* or what we *feel* but rather by who we *are* in Christ. After all, we are human *beings*, not human *doings*. Yet our tendency, even as Christians, is to find our identity in what we do.

We know this tendency well. When we played professional baseball, our identities were wrapped up in our careers as pro ball players. What we did defined who we were. But this was an outside-in approach to life. We badly needed to reverse that line of thinking and adopt the inside-out approach that Jesus had.

When asked if He was God's Son, Jesus replied, "I told you, and you do not believe; the works that I do in My Father's name, these *testify* of Me" (John 10:25). Notice Jesus said His works *testify* of Him; they did not *determine* Him. His actions attested to an identity already resolved in His heart. In fact, Jesus' ministry did not begin until His Father declared, "You are My beloved Son" (Mark 1:11). From that foundation alone, Jesus went forth to perform His Father's work. He first settled who He was. His actions then flowed naturally out of that identity. Jesus lived from the inside out, setting an example for all of us to follow.

 As Christians, we should find our identity in who we are, not what we do. Yet what we do will always flow out of who we are. This is the key to inside-out living.

Daniel and Jesus did not allow their positions or pay to define their identities. The same should apply to us. Position and pay can change, and so do our feelings, which come and go.

Moods also come and go, and insecurities will rise up and choke us, but Jesus is the same yesterday, today, and forever. He is our Rock, keeping us grounded in Him despite what we feel or what we do. But if our identity changes with our feelings, that means we had no true identity to begin with. If, however, we find our identity in the unchanging God, not only can we remain secure when the world changes, but we will have the power to transform our world.

RELIGION VERSUS RELATIONSHIP

One of the key hindrances to Christians possessing their identity is their tendency to be "religious." In December 2012, Gallup released findings from a survey showing that seven in ten Americans consider themselves "very or moderately religious." Yet within this same group, there are also alarmingly high numbers for depression, suicide, and other life-threatening or quality-of-life issues. Religion isn't offering answers for the problems of today.[4]

The word *religion* once referred to something positive—genuine faith and good works. But today it refers more often to outward spiritual practices devoid of a personal connection to God Himself. So people can be "religious" without having an actual relationship with God. They can attend a certain church, adhere to its teachings, observe some of its customs, give money, and perhaps even do some good works, but still lack an actual relationship with God.

Religion, then, enables people to feel as though they are Christians without actually transforming their identities. This is a systemic problem because God's power is then blocked from flowing out of their lives—the kind of power only those in relationship with Him possess. So when the test comes in Babylon, people without a true identity in Christ will not be able to stand with courage.

Daniel was not able to deny the king's food and deflect the king's praise because he was a "good ol' religious boy." Rather, he had a genuine relationship with God that gave him a deep sense of his own identity. No matter what threatened him, he would stay true to his identity as God's man in Babylon.

Religion transforms no one. However, "if anyone is in Christ, he is a new creature; the old things passed away; behold, new things have come" (2 Corinthians 5:17). A relationship with God, through faith in Christ, changes us from the inside out, giving us our new, true identity in Christ. Now God has called us to see ourselves in that new identity, rather than our old one. Then, just like Daniel, our new identity gives birth to powerful actions.

> To live among lions, who you are must come from who He is.

Once you are a child of God, it's like His identity is in your DNA. When you recognize this truth, a life of power and faithfulness is in your grasp.

RUN TO THE ROAR

When you see yourself for who you truly are, this sets the stage for you to see the world for what it truly is. And, as did the young lion, you will go back and take over the Father's kingdom—your world that God has destined you to transform. No more sitting in a worry-free zone because there is a very real enemy who seeks to "steal and kill and destroy" (John 10:10). The Devil knows one very important fact: how you see yourself determines how you conduct yourself. So if he can rob you of your identity, then he's well on his way to killing you and destroying everything you stand for.

But this doesn't have to happen. We hope you'll let us be the "baboons" that will help you see that your heavenly Father lives in you! Now go—run to the roar of those lions!

CHAPTER 3

THINK YOUR IDENTITY

And do not be conformed to this world, but be transformed by the renewing of your mind.

—ROMANS 12:2

 Even the strongest man alive remains a wimp as long as he believes he is. Thinking strong leads to being strong.

BABYLON'S KING COULD STRIP Daniel of his family and homeland, even plant him in foreign soil, but he could not strip him of his God-given identity. How did Daniel stand so strong? How was he able to maintain his identity as God's man amid the pressure to conform to the ways of a pagan culture? And how can we stand just as strong? Our culture is more aggressive than ever about redefining not just our basic laws and morals but Christianity in general.

We find the answer to these questions in the verse quoted at the beginning of this chapter. Daniel did more than just *accept* his identity as a Jew; he *determined to think like a Jew*—even in Babylon. Daniel was able to act like God's child because he determined to think like God's child.

The danger of religion is it inspires people to claim their identities as "Christians" while they continue to think exactly like the rest of the world. But what good does that do? Religious people do not intimidate the powers of darkness. Those powers couldn't care less about you *claiming* Christ if you don't *walk* in His power. This is one of the reasons we wrote this book. Churches have many people attending but too few of them transforming. We hear lots of sermons on being personally happy and successful, but too few of us are actually *thinking with the mind of Christ.*

 Outward affiliation never equals inward transformation.

Daniel was not a Jew by race and association only. He determined to *be* a Jew—God's man—in the center of his being. Check out what Paul said about this: "For he is not a Jew who is one outwardly, nor is circumcision that which is outward in the flesh. But he is a Jew who is one inwardly" (Romans 2:28–29).

This is why we love Daniel's example! He did not just claim to be God's man in Babylon; he consistently *thought* like God's man in Babylon. And this gave him the courage to live like God's man—anywhere. There's no way Daniel could have brought change as a resident of a pagan culture without thinking like a true citizen of heaven. His transforming actions flowed out of the thoughts of his renewed mind.

The same goes for you. God hasn't given you a new identity

just so you can squeak by in life, hold down a decent job, make a little money, and hopefully make it to heaven one day—not just so you can become the "best *you* that you can be" as though He's some motivational life coach. God has given you a new identity to put you in the business of changing the world for His glory!

Let's define two terms before going any further:

Transformers: Christ-followers, empowered by the Holy Spirit, who know their God, know *who* they are, *why* they're here, and *what* they're doing in the world. A transformer thinks according to God's pattern.

Conformers: People (Christian or not) who *find* their identity in the world, *feed* on the lies of man, *fit* into culture's mold, and *function* as society demands. A conformer can only think according to the patterns of the world.

We cannot transform our world unless we ourselves are transformed by the renewing of our minds. That is why Satan works so hard to attack the minds of Christians. He knows that in Christ, we are transformers by nature. But if we don't *think* like transformers, we will simply act like conformers.

Just because we initially embrace our newly transformed identities in Christ doesn't mean we automatically think like transformed people. It takes time for our minds to catch up. The Devil knows this, so he pushes hard for us to keep thinking like conformers.

Our thoughts, then, must begin to flow out of our identity in Christ. Transformational thinking precedes transformational living—from the inside out. This is where a conflict arises today in Christian circles. Many professing believers are essentially functional atheists. Why? Because they don't think in terms of their actual identity in Christ, and, tragically, they still allow the world to define them—being conformed to its patterns. It's easier to think in terms of our personal interests rather than to think like Christ—as if everyone else is more important than us (Philippians 2:3–11). It's easier to remain in the mind-set of profit and pleasure than it is to think first in terms of what honors God (Matthew 6:33). Transforming, on the other hand, takes commitment, work, and total reliance on the grace of God.

CONCRETE EVIDENCE

As teenagers growing up in Dallas, we would spend the hot summer months working outside all day long. For a few weeks one summer, we helped a friend form and pour concrete, which is not a job for the faint of heart. (*David: I constantly had to drag Jason along to keep up.*)

On one particular job, we were putting in a pool. Our main responsibility was to build the forms—the wooden borders for the concrete—to shape the sidewalks and the surrounding deck. This was a nightmare of a project. Although working with concrete in the blistering Texas heat pales in comparison to getting thrown into a fiery furnace, it's still a painful experience.

We gathered all our materials and went to work on the forms. When we were done, the truck rolled up and poured in the concrete. It flowed into the frames and filled out the pattern. At the end of the project, we had a sidewalk, surrounding deck, and pool shaped exactly according to the design.

The world wants us to *conform*. But God wants us to *transform* so we can make a difference in this world.

Aside from trying to sneak our handprints into the wet concrete, we learned a valuable lesson later in life through this experience. The world has built forms, designed for us to conform to, and if we're not proactively fighting against them, then we'll be shaped by them. Building God-honoring forms in our lives, according to His pattern, is vital to living a Daniel-life in Babylon.

INDOCTRI-NATION

When Daniel and his friends arrived in Babylon, there was a form into which they were to be poured. The king of Babylon brought these Jewish teens into his custody so he could fully indoctrinate them into the ways of Babylon. The king didn't want Jewish-thinking people in his court. He wanted Babylonian-thinking people, coupled with the excellence of their Jewish roots. So what did the king need to do to accomplish this?

+ Phase One: Cultivate a taste for the things of Babylon.
+ Phase Two: Create a paradigm toward the thinking of Babylon.

The king wanted specifically to get these kids to . . .

+ want Babylonian things,
+ think Babylonian thoughts,

- see the Babylonian ways,
- acquire Babylonian desires,
- possess Babylonian paradigms,
- embrace Babylonian gods, and
- conform to Babylonian patterns.

Does that list remind you of the cultural indoctrination going on today? We have allowed ourselves to cultivate appetites for the things of this world, yet we still want to be transformers for God. The two cannot go hand in hand.

Daniel's refusal to conform had to begin right at the point when he was presented with the first bite of the king's food. He knew if he lost the battle over his appetite, the process of conforming to their culture would begin.

 Kids need to hear this today: if they learn to say no now, when their bodies say yes, then it will be much easier for them to courageously say no later, when their culture demands they say yes.

At many of our universities today, young people are being indoctrinated into the ways of a godless world for at least four years, which is actually one year longer than Daniel was trained in Babylon. By the time many of them leave college, they have appetites for the things of the world and hold fast to paradigms that are not only devoid of God but often hostile toward Him.

Thank God for Daniel and his friends being willing to transform and not conform so we have a strong example to follow today. They refused to be poured into the forms of Babylon. Although outwardly they mixed in, inwardly they maintained their God-honoring form (remember the chocolate chips). These boys weren't trying to change anything. They were just living transformed lives right where God had placed them and refused to think like their culture. They didn't take even a bite of that food.

Such transformational living must begin with renewed thinking. To renew our minds means to replace our old thoughts with new thoughts. These new thoughts come from God's Word and are truth—about God and our identity in Him. The old thoughts come from the Enemy and reflect the patterns of the world. They are lies about God and our identity in Him (John 8:42–47).

When my (David's) wife, Lori, wants to change her fingernail polish, she has to first remove the old and then put on the new. If she just tries to slap the new over the old, it will peel, and she hates it when her nail polish peels. This is a simple analogy of renewal.

But we cannot simply try to think differently. Paul didn't tell us in the Romans passage to pray longer, try harder, or do better—but to put on the new mind in and from God's Word. The only way to dislodge lies deeply ingrained in our thinking is through the power of God's Word. (More on this in a later chapter.)

This process of renewal has two crucial components and action steps:

1. Renounce

    The old thoughts that conform us to the world are lies we believe to be true. So we begin renewing our minds by such thoughts. To renounce is "to give up, refuse, or resign usually by formal declaration" or "to refuse to follow, obey, or recognize any further."[1] So when you recognize a thought pattern that contradicts God's Word—a pattern you have owned in your mind—then renounce it. Confess the lie, formally declare your abandonment of the thought, and stop using it.

For example, if you have been taught your faith is only a private matter with no bearing on public life, you must renounce that lie and prepare to replace it with a new thought pattern. Or maybe you view God as an angry judge or absentee father rather than a faithful, loving Father. This is another false notion that has the power to infect your emotions and actions. Target *your* ideas and renounce them!

Renouncing the lies you've believed is a powerful component to your personal transformation. You must first remove the lies before you can put on the new truth from God. This leads to the second step.

2. Replace

We cannot merely renounce old thoughts and expect our minds to be renewed. God's truth must replace the lie so the Enemy can't put another one of his back in its place. That's when the force of God's Word floods our brainwaves, renews our minds, and makes us powerful people. But we cannot be lazy about this step. We must be deliberate—laser-focused and aggressive.

In Matthew 12 and Luke 11, Jesus taught about when an evil spirit leaves a person, he may return and find "it unoccupied, swept, and put in order" (Matthew 12:44). Then he returns and brings seven friends, making the person's final condition far worse than before. Wait! What? But the house was unoccupied, swept clean, and in order. Exactly! It was clean, but the truth of God was not put in its place, so there was plenty of empty space for the Enemy to move right back in and bring his buddies. Replacement is just as crucial as renouncement. Jesus said so!

Find Bible verses that specifically contradict the lies you've believed, and make those words your new thoughts. For example, maybe you believe our culture is too far gone, beyond the reach of Christian influence, so all you can do is sit quietly on the sidelines and wait for Christ to return. That kind of thinking is a lie from the Enemy that must be replaced with a verse like Daniel 11:32: "But the people who know their God will display strength and take action." Such a statement reveals God's way of thinking—the kind we need in our minds while living in a pagan culture.

 Renouncing Satan's lies and replacing them with God's truth brings renewal.

So be intentional to replace the world's lies with specific truths from God's Word. Christians cannot just try to un-think the old. They *must deliberately think the way God thinks.* And He has provided His thoughts for us in the Bible, revealed to our hearts by the Holy Spirit.

Your word I have treasured in my heart,
That I may not sin against You.

—PSALM 119:11

MESSIANIC MOUTHWASH

Growing up, we were two of the most competitive kids around. (You're not surprised, are you?) Rarely did we play in the fourth quarter of a basketball game. We were usually on the bench— fouled out. Our aggression was beyond that of normal teenagers. In particular, I (Jason) struggled with my mouth. I'm not saying I would blurt out obscenities in the middle of a game or anything. But if I fouled out, I would say words under my breath that would not make my mama proud. Although I had become a Christian at twelve years old, my mind—and therefore my mouth—had not yet caught up with that new identity. My actions were not yet in line with who I was because my thinking wasn't being renewed. I had a new identity, but I was not yet *incorporating* that identity into my thinking. I was not yet renewing my mind.

Even though I was reading my Bible every morning, in the moments when a bad word would come to my mind, I wasn't proactively renouncing and replacing it with the truth of God's Word. I had to learn that renewal was a process—something I needed to continually do in my mind.

I remember confessing to Dad that I was struggling with my mouth and feeling as though this was impossible to overcome. He told me something I have never forgotten: "The warfare for your soul takes place on the battleground of your mind."

He then took me to Luke 4 and showed me how Jesus over-came Satan's temptations through God's Word. He explained that each time I let a bad word fly, I was believing a lie of Satan. For me, the lie was thinking that if I uttered a curse word, I would relieve the anger of losing or fouling out. But the truth was, my words reflected what was in my heart. Giving them voice did not bring relief. In the long run, they only fueled more frustration and broke my fellowship with God.

So I needed to renew my mind in order to transform my mouth. (Now, if David could have only found something to transform his hairstyle in high school—he used to look like Vanilla Ice!)

Dad then encouraged me to memorize a few verses of truth that would expose the lie. He coached me to recite them over and over, anytime I felt the urge to let loose. He knew the power of God's Word in my mouth would eventually activate renewal in my mind.

I remember thinking, *Yeah, right, like that's going to work.* But even though I didn't really feel like it, I did it anyway. I was desperate and didn't want to conform anymore—I really wanted to transform.

The best place for me to try this out was with David on the battleground. (I mean, in the backyard.) We played every possible sport in our yard: basketball, baseball, boxing, and football. So this seemed the most appropriate place to tackle this battle of the mind. As much as I struggled with my mouth, David couldn't control his temper. Putting us together in heated competition was like combining nitro and glycerin—an explosion was usually on the way. I would use my mouth to rile him up, then sit back and watch the fireworks. I knew this was wrong, but it just felt so right.

A quick side note here I just can't pass up—David lost control during one of those boxing matches. As his anger got the best of him, he drew back to throw a massive overhand right. But during his windup, I threw a small jab square to his chin and dropped him like a bag of bricks. When he regained consciousness, he started screaming, "All I see is green!" It was the most absolutely amazing feeling a boy could have—especially against his twin brother and archrival. My eyes still well up with tears of joy thinking about that moment.

But enough about David's chin and back to my mouth.

The minute I decided I wanted to do something about my bad language, everything got harder. David's fouls against me in basketball got worse. I struck out more. I lost more races. The temptations seemed to get bigger, not smaller. You know the feeling?

But I decided to go for it all the more. I was determined to be proactive about renewing my mind. So each time I went up for a shot and got mauled by my brother (the only way he could defend me), I would clinch my fists, grit my teeth, and quote Ephesians 4:29: "Let no unwholesome word proceed from your mouth." Most of the time I forgot the rest of the verse, so I would use the half I knew. (Sorry, Dad.)

I would say the verse again and again despite how angry I was. I didn't win every battle at first. But guess what started to happen over time? Slowly I began to win more here and there until my mouth was totally clean.

My victory, however, was not just over my mouth. The bad language had been flowing out of my heart. So Dad's advice about memorizing and speaking God's Word did more than give me a new, outward habit. It enabled me to renounce the lie in my mind and replace it with God's truth as a way of thinking. "He who believes in Me, as the Scripture said, 'From his innermost being will flow rivers of living water'" (John 7:38).

After a process of devoting time and effort, the power of God's Word renewed my mind in that particular area. My old pattern of thinking had genuinely changed from a reaction of offensive words to a response of grace and patience. (Then I would calmly return to our game and destroy David.)

I was like a new man. My circumstances had not changed at all. David still mauled me. I was still tested during our backyard bouts and on the court. But everything inside had changed for me.

Here's what's really cool. When I got to the pros, by God's grace my speech was squeaky clean, even when the heat turned up. In the clubhouse, the players' language was really bad at times. Yet not only was I able to keep my speech clean, but other guys started to feel guilty about their own language when I was around. If they blurted out a cuss word and saw me close by, they would apologize. It was funny because I had never said a word to them about cussing. But my own speech was a rebuke, and the contrast brought conviction.

Like Daniel, I wasn't trying to change my environment in my own power. Rather, my renewed mind enabled me to *live* the change I had experienced earlier. Then, over time, the entire atmosphere of the clubhouse shifted. This was an amazing transformation to watch.

 Internal transformation precedes genuine external transformation. The river of holiness always flows from the inside out.

When we abandon the world's way of thinking and embrace God's way, no power on earth can stop the transformation. Not even the most powerful leader in the world. Daniel's life revealed this truth, and so can ours. Yet we must renew ourselves daily with God's way of thinking so we can transform our culture, not conform to it.

MAMMOTH MIND-SET

Do you know what circus workers do to keep their elephants from running away? They tie the mighty beasts to a small peg that's hammered into the ground.

At any moment, a hulking elephant can break the chain with his God-given strength and escape to freedom. But he never does. Why? When the elephant is a baby, the chain is too strong to break. When he becomes full-grown, he still thinks the chain can hold him—he can't escape to freedom. He stays locked in bondage even though he now has the strength to break free easily. This also can be done to adult elephants if left chained long enough and they hurt themselves trying to break free. Eventually they give up, yielding to their bondage.

This is the power of thinking in terms of our identity in Christ. God has destined us to transform our world, and He's given us the strength to do so. But we must start thinking in terms of who we are in Him—free from the bondage of our old ways of thinking. And when we forget, all we've got to do is jump back into His Word so He can remind us how strong we truly are in Him. This new mind-set will then radically change how we view our world and fuel our thoughts to bring true transformation.

CHAPTER 4

BUILD YOUR WORLDVIEW

The earth is the LORD's, and all it contains.

—PSALM 24:1

 Even the tiniest things are meaning*full* when you see as God sees—even the biggest things are meaning*less* when you don't.

HAVE YOU EVER SEEN a 3-D random dot stereogram? Yeah, we know, *stereogram* is a pretty big word for guys like us, but it makes us feel smart to ask the question. Those are the pictures made up of thousands of tiny dots that make up a 3-D image. The kicker is you can't see the image on the surface. You can only see it if your eyes adjust and look at the picture from the right perspective. It takes time for your sight to settle into the accurate viewpoint, and until you do, the stereogram just looks like a bunch of dots. But when you finally catch the right view and see the hidden image—it's like an epiphany! Suddenly you see the picture clearly. Once you do, then you can't *not* see it.

When we were kids, a family in our church gave Dad a stereogram for his birthday. They were so excited and told him they couldn't wait for him to see the picture. For several days, Dad couldn't see anything but a bunch of dots. Every day he'd pick up the stereogram and stare, yet he saw nothing. Then one day, through the sea of dots, he saw it. The image jumped right out at him—Jesus on the cross. Dad said the picture was so powerful he felt as though he got saved all over again.

But the picture had not changed. Dad's *perspective* changed. His eyes finally settled into the right point of view so he could see the clear image in all the dots. Every time he looked at the picture from that day on, he could see Jesus. We remember looking at it too, but we never once saw the image. We were too busy boxing with each other in the backyard to stare at a picture. But Dad took the time necessary to see Jesus in what looked like only a sea of dots to us.

God wants to give us all the eyes to see His Son, Jesus, amid the dots of life. He calls us to see the world from His perspective. For this to occur, we must have a biblical worldview. When we view the world the way God does, everything in life begins to make sense. Then we finally see as He sees. We clearly witness His hand at work in the world while others can't seem to make out what is actually going on in the big picture. Without this worldview, even if we claim to be Christians, we cannot live with the conviction to withstand the pressure so we can transform our world.

Here's what Chuck Colson wrote concerning a biblical worldview:

> Genuine Christianity is more than a relationship with Jesus, as expressed in personal piety, church attendance, Bible study, and works of charity. It is more than discipleship, more

than believing a system of doctrines about God. Genuine Christianity is a way of seeing and comprehending *all* reality. It is a worldview.[1]

In this chapter we're taking personal transformation to the next level. Our relationship with God, as well as our perception of ourselves, must now expand into our view of the world. This is a central theme in the book of Daniel. From the personal stories in the first half to the prophecies in the second half, Daniel's story is all about viewing life and history from God's perspective—that is, from the viewpoint of God's kingdom.

With this perspective, nothing will shake us.

The same truth that determined Daniel's identity and the patterns of his thinking also defined his entire world. That was how he could remain faithful to God in Babylon.

BATTING 1,000 IN BABYLON

One reason Daniel and his friends remained faithful even to the point of death—and were able to transform their world—is they had a biblical worldview. To them, the world was not ruled by Nebuchadnezzar and centered on Babylon; the world was ruled by God and centered on His kingdom.

Maintaining such a worldview took major faith and courage. The land of Israel and the temple in Jerusalem were powerful physical symbols of the Jews' faith in God. God gave them the promised land and dwelled in their temple, and both were significant to their faith. These things were also a sign that God was the Lord of all creation and all nations.

So what happened when those things were taken away— sacred things that so deeply confirmed their worldview? Now, living in a foreign land that worshipped false gods under the rule of a pagan king, was their God still sovereign? Was it possible to maintain their worldview and be faithful while in Babylon? Was it even worth doing?

The book of Daniel tackles these very questions. And Daniel himself provides the answers—both for the exiled Jews of his day and for us as well. He was able to see the image of God's kingdom among a sea of Babylonian "dots." His scenery changed, but his worldview did not. So he ordered his life accordingly.

This is exactly why this is called a worldview. Your *view* remains consistent no matter what takes place in your *world*. Daniel maintained his conviction that "the earth is the LORD's" and *everything* in it (Psalm 24:1). Despite judgment and dramatically changing circumstances, the God of Israel was still God. Babylon's dominion did not change that fact.

Daniel and his friends proved that Jews could still be faithful to God and their own identity even during exile—even when major outward signs of God's sovereignty were taken away from them, as their temple was destroyed and they were deported from their land. In its entirety, the book of Daniel is a declaration that if God's people maintained their kingdom worldview in Babylon, then they would be the symbol of that kingdom anywhere on earth. How cool is that?

What about today? As God's people in America, we tie much of our worldview to outward symbols. More often than we care to admit, our view of God's sovereignty is attached to church buildings, successful ministry careers, large conferences, celebrity leaders, and even tax-exempt status. But what happens if all these are taken away? Is God still the King? Does heaven still rule? Will we still be faithful? Asked another way, is our worldview larger than just *our* world?

We believe Nebuchadnezzar's first dream—where God revealed that His kingdom would trump all other kingdoms and fill the whole earth—was not just for him but also for God's people in Babylon and for *us*. The message to us all is that God's kingdom is and always will be sovereign, even in a world that seems to be dominated by other kingdoms. *His* kingdom is the Rock that fills the earth—and will fill the earth. Daniel's interpretation was that God's kingdom reigns regardless of who rules temporarily in the physical realm (Daniel 2:35–38).

After God gave him the first interpretation, Daniel proclaimed, "It is He who changes the times and the epochs; He removes kings and establishes kings" (v. 21). God showed Daniel what his worldview should be even while exiled in Babylon—and nothing would shake him from that. God revealed this truth to Daniel through the "dots" of the dream: Nebuchadnezzar did not make himself king; God did. The God of heaven raised him up and would bring him down.

So even if evil would prevail to a degree for a time, Daniel still saw the 3-D image of God's kingdom and never lost sight of it. Daniel's worldview told him God was *always* the sovereign Lord of the world; history belonged to Him. Babylon did not change this truth.

In fact, Daniel's God-centered worldview made him the most valuable man in Babylon's kingdom. He became the one from whom the king sought answers to his most difficult questions. Daniel's faith went beyond having a kosher diet and keeping the Sabbath. He possessed a total life system that motivated his every action. As a result, God allowed him to interpret mysteries no one else could.

On multiple occasions, Daniel was brought before troubled kings who couldn't see through all the "dots." Nebuchadnezzar had perplexing dreams that made no sense to him (Daniel 2 and 4). He knew the dreams had meaning, but he needed someone with eyes to see. The next king, Belshazzar, saw a physical hand write an inscription on the wall that no one could read or interpret (Daniel 5). In each instance, Daniel brought clarity where there was confusion.

I CAN SEE CLEARLY NOW

Christianity isn't just a religion or another belief system, but it's a comprehensive worldview that has the answers to life's questions and brings tangible solutions to the problems in our world. Following Christ with our minds, not just our hearts, helps us see the big picture in the matrix of dots. Christianity is a total life system that first transforms *us* and then transforms the world around us. Yet so many Christians don't seem to catch this truth. All they see are the dots, never seeing their place in the world as God truly intended.

Chuck Colson explained it this way:

Understanding Christianity as a total life system is absolutely essential, for two reasons. First, it enables us to make sense of the world we live in and thus order our lives more rationally. Second, it enables us to understand forces hostile to our faith, equipping us to evangelize and to defend Christian truth as God's instruments for transforming culture.[2]

Our world today just doesn't make sense outside of a biblical worldview. Explaining to our kids why some men are trying to become women, why certain people despise the Judeo-Christian foundation of our country, or how Christian values have been twisted into a new narrative and called "hate" is otherwise impossible. Our biblical worldview provides a stable and never-changing standard that enables us to make sense of the moral madness and equip the next generation to transform their world in Christian love.

Failure to see Christianity as a total life system has led many in the church to sit quietly on the sidelines. Many professing Christians tolerate the blatant erosion of morals in culture, and at times some even celebrate them. But how can the one institution ordained by God to transform the world sit out when the stakes are so high?

When we were kids, Dad decided to move his pastor's office right next door to one of the busiest abortion clinics in Dallas. The facility turned out to be owned by the infamous "Jane Roe" of the *Roe v. Wade* Supreme Court decision that had legalized abortion (we'll use her actual name, Norma). People thought our dad was nuts to do this, but he saw through the dots. While so many viewed Norma as the enemy, Dad saw her simply as someone God loved.

He would tell us, "Boys, my goal is not just to end abortion, but first to advance God's kingdom. Ms. Norma needs Jesus, and we have the answer!"

Not long after Dad moved next door, he befriended Norma, and his secretary started taking cookies over to her at the abortion clinic. How cool is that? Eventually, Norma and her lesbian partner were sitting at our dining room table, enjoying dinner with our family. Through this newfound relationship, both of them prayed to receive Christ. Dad baptized Norma in our friends' swimming pool. We still remember all the news outlets there filming the event. They were all baffled at how kind Dad and Norma were to each other. When the world could only see dots, Dad, again, saw Jesus. And our family got a front-row seat to watch God's transforming power at work in the midst of a deeply entrenched cultural and political battle.

This was the first situation where Dad taught us to see past the *issue* that divides us to the *person* God loves. In the same way, Daniel never made Babylon's kings his enemies. A biblical worldview gives us the supernatural ability to see people through God's eyes, with unconditional love.

LAY LOW OR STAND UP

One week after we got the boot from reality TV, we received some surprising advice from a respected Christian leader. He told us, "If you guys can just quiet down a bit and lay low, then you can protect your image and possibly land another reality show. Maybe you can regain a platform to proclaim the gospel." While we can honestly say, prior to getting fired, we were tempted to sit on the sidelines in order to protect our image, we had seen God's hand at work behind the scenes and were ready to take a stand.

How were we supposed to keep quiet when we were given an

opportunity to speak the truth? As Rick Johnson wrote, "When men stand on the sidelines with hands in pockets and faces downcast in shame—as Adam once did—all good things die."[3] We weren't about to sit quietly by as spectators and let "good things die."

While our leader friend only saw the dots of culture, God helped us see a clear picture of His cross—the way of His kingdom—in the midst of our situation. We knew instantly God was telling us to pick up our cross and carry it. He had granted us eyes to see, and in that moment our spiritual vision was twenty-twenty. Our worldview directed and drove our actions.

We knew this was *not* the time to protect our image, but it was high time to stand and "defend Christian truth as God's instruments for transforming culture," as Chuck Colson had said.

Actually, we had fifty-twenty vision in this moment (Genesis 50:20). When Joseph revealed himself to his brothers many years after they sold him into slavery, he told them, "As for you, you meant evil against me, but God meant it for good in order to bring about this present result, to preserve many people alive." It's this type of vision that allows you to live faithfully in a darkening culture.

WAR OF THE WORLDS

Everyone today is either leading or being led. We are either advancing onward or sliding backward, contributing to the broken condition of the world or bringing about its healing. Whether we realize it or not, every person has a worldview. We all have a lens through which we view life that morphs and changes regularly throughout childhood and early adulthood but, at some point, lands on a set way to approach existence.

 A biblical worldview takes your faith and makes it a lens through which you filter all of life so you can live faithfully.

There will always be an opposing worldview that will clash with the biblical worldview. When these collide—as they have since the beginning of time—the end result is often persecution for the people of God. "Indeed, all who desire to live godly in Christ Jesus will be persecuted" (2 Timothy 3:12). Our focus must not be on eliminating or escaping persecution but on living faithfully for God—seeking to see as He sees with a succinct worldview that points directly to Christ in all situations.

There is a clear battle today between opposing worldviews, each vying for control of the planet. As the Bible states in Genesis 3:15, there are two "seeds"—the seed of the woman (Jesus) and the seed of the serpent (Satan). The battle we fight is over who is Lord and whose laws reign. There is no compromise between the two. No neutrality. Choose one or the other.

Jesus made this point quite clear in Matthew 12:30: "He who is not with Me is against Me; and he who does not gather with Me scatters."

 If you straddle the fence, you'll tear the seat of your pants.

The seed of Satan says, "I am the center of my universe—my rights, my body, my choice. I'm here to satisfy myself and do what makes me happy in life, marriage, sex, and all choices." Various worldviews actually develop from this one mind-set, but they all share the common root of humanism (being man-centered). The exception to this would be other religions that hold to the concept of God but ultimately deny the seed of God (Jesus).

The seed of God (Jesus) says, "God is the center of my universe. Even as God's child, I am not entitled to insist on my rights [Philippians 2:6]. I am here to serve the Father's interests, not my own. I am most fulfilled when I do His will [John 4:34]." As Jesus' followers, that same seed abides in us, so we share the same biblical worldview (being God-centered).

At its root, humanism places man at the center of the universe. Biblical Christianity, however, places God at the center of the universe. Humanism allows for gods, but they must fit into "my" picture. In Christianity, we fit into God's picture.

In Daniel's story we see a cataclysmic clash between these worldviews. As Nebuchadnezzar proudly walked on the roof of his royal palace, his humanist worldview—and the predictable consequences—was on full display for all to see:

> The king reflected and said, "Is this not Babylon the great, which I myself have built as a royal residence by the might of my power for the glory of my majesty?" While the word was in the king's mouth, a voice came from heaven, saying, "King Nebuchadnezzar, to you it is declared: sovereignty has been removed from you, and you will be driven away from mankind, and your dwelling place will be with the beasts of the field . . . until you recognize that the Most High is the ruler over the realm of mankind and bestows on it whomever He wishes."
>
> —DANIEL 4:30–32

Tell me that wouldn't freak you out! This is one of the most powerful examples in history of worldviews clashing —and guess who won? God did. He always does. Humanism cannot stand up to the living God.

Unfortunately many people today profess to be Christians but don't have a biblical worldview and, thus, get "tossed here and there by waves" of the culture (Ephesians 4:14). Still thinking like humanists, they want God for *eternal* life, but they choose to leave themselves at the center of their *daily* life. Therefore, they divide their lives into separate compartments: sacred and secular.

How do we say this version of the faith is whacked without our mom thinking we're too harsh?

At an 1820 celebration of the Pilgrims' landing at Plymouth Rock, Daniel Webster, legendary senator, statesman, and secretary of state, said, "Let us not forget the religious character of our origin. Our fathers were brought hither by their high veneration for the Christian religion. They journeyed by its light and labored in its hope. They sought to incorporate its principles with the elements of their society, and to diffuse its influence through all their institutions, civil, political, or literary."[4]

 With a biblical worldview, separating our lives and the surrounding culture into sacred and secular compartments is impossible.

So many of our forefathers and founding fathers had a biblical worldview, which led them to build a nation *under God*. Though they were far from perfect, they still understood that "The earth is the LORD's, and all it contains" (Psalm 24:1). If the earth is the Lord's, then *everything* is under God—all areas and institutions of life are meant to be under His dominion (family, church, government, marketplace, law, science, education, media—everything).

To bring this idea home, take out a sheet of paper and draw a line down the middle from top to bottom. On one side list areas of life that God cares about, and on the other side list those He doesn't care about. Get the point? God cares for everything in this world because it's *His* world.

For America to return to the blessing of her heritage, we must return to a biblical worldview.

Most Americans, unfortunately, believe in the sacred-secular divide. Check out a few alarming statistics from George Barna that help explain the moral slide we're experiencing today: only 7 to 9 percent of people possess the same Judeo-Christian worldview of our founding fathers, yet close to 83 percent of Americans believe themselves to be Christian.[5] This should not be. The time has come to begin seeing as God sees, to possess a biblical worldview and become God's instruments of transformation—just as Daniel was.

CONNECTING THE DOTS

We were asked to sit on a panel where we would be interviewed by a well-known conservative talk-show host in Dallas. There was also an influential writer on the panel with us, so we were outsmarted all the way around (which is not hard to do). When the host asked what we believed to be the problem with society today, the writer gave a long answer that was rooted in policy and filled with conservative jargon.

When it was our turn to respond, I (Jason) responded first (which is unusual for me): "We have a theology problem in America, and until we get right with God, all our creative conservative policies are going to amount to a hot, steaming cup of jack-squat!"

The crowd erupted in applause and laughter. Drop the mic. Slow clap. That one felt good. It was obviously God because I blurted the words out without even thinking first. I went on to talk about the clash of worldviews and how this battle is nothing new today. I spoke about our lack of a biblical worldview and how knowledge of God has all but disappeared from the nation.

David then explained how Christians could live faithfully within a biblical framework in every sphere of life. He pointed out that we should not be dividing our lives into sacred or secular compartments. The crowd erupted again (but David's response didn't get the laughter, so he couldn't drop the mic).

There we were, just two business guys without a political bone in our bodies, standing on stage at a high-profile event, talking to people who were considered some of America's top conservative thinkers. And yet when we simply boiled it down to living faithfully within a biblical worldview, where God is supreme, the truth connected with the crowd instantly. The people were so hungry for this simple truth; it reminded us of a verse in Proverbs: "But to a famished man any bitter thing is sweet" (27:7).

Our nation is starving, dying, for believers with a biblical worldview who are willing to live out their faith in every sphere of life. People don't need just another political strategy. They want clarity instead of confusion, like the clarity Daniel brought to Babylon. Americans don't need another cool message on how to have a better life—they want answers to life's most pressing problems.

A biblical worldview is the only way to deliver these solutions.

When asked about the importance of a biblical worldview, we usually respond with a simple story of two men who are mixing concrete on a job site in New York City. As you approach the first man and ask what he's doing, he simply responds, "I'm mixing concrete." Yet when you approach the second man and ask the same question, he stops working and points behind him, saying, "I'm building a skyscraper." Both men are doing the same job, but only one man views his job properly. When the hard times come—which they will—only those "building a skyscraper" won't quit and walk away. They'll persevere, knowing there's a much greater purpose for their lives.

If you find yourself just mixing concrete in life, it's time to stop and look up. See how your life fits into God's plan, and check if you view the world as He does. Then realize that one of the secrets to having a biblical worldview is to simply *re-view* God's plan in His Word every single day. This has been our habit since we were twelve years old, and we hope you make it yours too.

CHAPTER 5

CHOOSE REVERENCE

Establish Your word to Your servant,
As that which produces reverence for You.

—Psalm 119:38

 Relevance is a by-product of reverence. If you want to be relevant to culture, you must first be reverent to God.

FOR THE PAST FEW years, *relevance* has become a buzzword in many Christian circles. The big question many churches and Christian leaders are asking is, "How can we be more relevant to the surrounding culture and still maintain our convictions to God?" We hear this question quite often.

To be blunt, this mind-set is shortsighted and weak. There's nothing wrong with being relevant—it's actually a good thing— but it must not be our main focus as Christians. Focusing on relevance causes us to judge the effectiveness of a ministry more by the number of people it draws than by real devotion to God.

This lacks spiritual strength and leads to politically correct posturing rather than true biblical leadership. We don't believe Daniel would have ever dreamed of asking questions like this. And neither should we today. As this way of thinking was completely outside the scope of his identity and worldview, so it should be outside of ours. We need to be asking, "How can we be reverent to God?" Then leave the relevance to Him.

Reverence means fearing God and not man—worshipping, respecting, seeking to please and honor Him above any other consideration. An attitude of reverence is part of our inner transformation—our conviction.

Daniel was one reverent dude. He made decisions solely based on his fear of God, like avoiding the king's food, thus risking his life; continuing to pray even though he knew the punishment; and confronting the king when his position was on the line. Daniel shows us how to make decisions based on the fear of God and not the fear of man.

> The fear of man brings a snare,
> But he who trusts in the LORD will be exalted.
> —PROVERBS 29:25

This single verse sums up Daniel's testimony. His reverence paved the way for his relevance, and he was able to meet the real, spiritual needs of the people around him.

Daniel and his friends knew the same God who transformed them from the inside out was the only God to whom they would ever bow. No matter what happened in Babylon, they would remain true to this conviction. God was their life, so He deserved their reverence.

When everyone did what was culturally relevant by bowing to Nebuchadnezzar's golden image in Daniel 3, Shadrach, Meshach, and Abed-nego did what was personally reverent by standing up, unwilling to break so they could fit in with everyone else. As a result, can you imagine all the conversations in Babylon about the three dudes in the fiery furnace—oh wait, make that four—who came out unharmed, not even smelling like smoke (vv. 25–27)? The city was probably buzzing with the hype. These guys were instantly the most relevant brothers in Babylon.

By refusing to kneel before the earthly king, they received the smile of their heavenly King. *Boom!*

Only a man whose heart is bowed in reverence would choose to stand on God's truth when the surrounding culture demands he bow. These boys properly understood their one duty was to remain reverent to God and allow Him to handle the results.

 Those who bow in reverence to God and leave the results to Him will become relevant in His time, in His way.

Daniel and his friends were armed with the stories of courageous people of God who chose to honor the Lord when everyone else was bowing at a different altar, and like them, these four men desired the hope of heaven rather than the cool of culture. They undoubtedly remembered men such as Noah, who lived centuries before them. Noah had chosen to obey God by building the ark even though he looked completely irrelevant, and possibly ridiculous, while doing so (Genesis 6).

Check out what the writer of Hebrews said about Noah:

> By faith Noah, being warned by God about things not yet seen, in *reverence* prepared an ark for the salvation of his household, by which he condemned the world, and became an heir of the righteousness which is according to faith.
>
> —HEBREWS 11:7

God told Noah rain was coming—but no one at that time had ever seen this natural force. Rain didn't exist yet! So for the next 120 years, Noah—in reverence—built an ark for the salvation of his family and, ultimately, the human race. Can you imagine how irrelevant he seemed during those 120 years?

"Hey, Noah! What are you doing?"

"I'm building an ark because God is going to bring rain and flood the earth."

"What's rain?"

"Water falling from the sky."

"You're an idiot!"

If Noah had focused on being relevant to his culture, then he would have never built the boat. Why? Because when your goal is relevance, you will focus more on strategy (doing what makes sense) than on the Spirit (doing what God commands).

 Christians should focus on the Spirit, doing what pleases God, before they focus on strategy, doing what makes sense to man.

But Noah focused on being reverent to God and faithfully obeying Him, regardless of how he would be perceived in his culture. He followed the Spirit of God and not the strategy of man.

He continued to operate in faith, not allowing his own understanding to be his guide.

> Trust in the LORD with all your heart
> And do not lean on your own understanding.
>
> —PROVERBS 3:5

But check this out—the minute the first drop of rain hit the ground, who do you think was the most relevant man on the planet?

MEASURING MOTIVES

What about us? Do the frowns of people scare us so much that we cannot focus on the face of God and act in simple obedience to His clear commands?

Relevance provides us with no absolute standard to measure our motives or actions. Reverence places God and His Word as the absolute standard by which all things are measured. Relevance puts *man* first, asking, "What do people think? What's popular? What's trending?" These aren't bad things to consider, but to live faithfully, we must never consider them first. Choosing relevance first is rooted in the fear of man. Reverence, on the other hand, considers *God* first, asking, "What does God think? What pleases Him? How would He have me act?" We need to ask these questions if we want to live faithfully.

Christians should never focus on the frowns of people but on the face of God.

Today, when we focus on being relevant, we find we become largely irrelevant. Why? Relevance is not what people need; they need the truth. They need ultimate answers as the flooding rains of culture pour down and pound away at their marriages, families, jobs, and health. Hurting people need God's authentic, tangible love, power, and kingdom—real spiritual solutions that can come only through reverent hearts. Only those who focus first on God with reverence will have an ark of safety to help them.

Although living like this is becoming increasingly unpopular, we must, like Daniel and Noah before him, choose reverence over relevance for God's kingdom to come.

POPULAR VERSUS POWERFUL

Choosing reverence can lead to conflict—a clash of opinions and a collision of worldviews. When the prevailing worldview of culture stands opposed to God and His Word, the truly reverent person *restates, reaffirms,* and *reapplies* biblical truth.[1]

Restate: What does the Bible say?
Reaffirm: I believe what the Bible says.
Reapply: I will apply what the Bible says to my life and culture.

This threefold focus puts to flight any cultural idea that stands opposed to God and His Word. The one who seeks only to remain relevant simply reconciles the Bible to the prevailing worldview, thus breaking God's truth down to the lowest common denominator. This is done for the sole purpose of everyone getting along and avoiding persecution. But this is not the way faithful people of God live with conviction.

Should the church water down the gospel message to satisfy the crowd in an effort to win people to Christ? If relevance is your deciding factor, then the answer is yes. In that case, we should try to be as relevant as we can, reconciling our biblical worldview with the surrounding culture and never allowing the gospel to be an offense.

But if reverence to God is leading our decisions in the church, then we should—as Daniel—lovingly deliver God's message of truth regardless of cost or consequence, letting relevance come or go as God desires. Because when the floodwaters of life start hitting the ground, the masses will return to where they know an ark has been built.

Living faithfully like this might not make us popular, but it will make us powerful.

 The same boiling water that hardens the egg softens the carrot. Don't focus on the temperature of the water but on the substance of what's in the water.

Consider the church in America today. Reverence to God has all but been swept under the rug to make the gospel more "relevant" and "attractive." Many churches spend more time and money on packaging the gospel than presenting the power of it. Oftentimes the focus is more on the container of Christianity than on its content. And Sunday sermons tend to avoid the issues instead of equipping the saints to navigate them. The church may have cool programs and services that attract seekers on a

Sunday, but there is little help to equip them for the battles they face on Monday. As a result, the institutions of culture (government, media, education, the marketplace) find little value in the Christian faith. Loss of reverence for God has brought a pervasive lack of respect for the church.

Yet the tide is turning as a remnant of believers around this nation are awakening to the fact that, while living reverently in America with the same conviction as Daniel in Babylon, their message is becoming very relevant. They have the answers that bring safety from the flooding rains—the truth that brings life—and are willing to speak without fear of being reviled, mocked, and ridiculed.

SAFE!

I (David) remember my early years of professional baseball when several of the guys would go out partying after games. Depending on the town we were in, various women (not from their families) would accompany some of them. Nothing good ever happened when those combinations were in play.

A few of my fellow players used to hound me to go with them, yet I never felt right about hitting the club scene just to be "one of the guys." Quite often, I wrestled in my mind if I should go to build relationships with them, but this particular situation never felt right. I knew there were plenty of other opportunities to hang with the guys without being in the middle of a smoky bar.

I wanted to be a relevant teammate, and I knew Jesus was a friend of sinners—but did I have to become *like* them to reach them? I had never experienced this before, and I spent hours in prayer to get an answer to this question.

Still, I never went.

Eventually I saw an interesting trend begin. I became the teammate the guys turned to when their lives fell apart—when the floodwaters started pouring in. Hearing a knock at my hotel room door at two in the morning was common for me, as a drunken teammate would bear his soul about his guilt and shame from doing things he knew were wrong. I counseled dozens of players when their marriages were falling apart, when a family member died, or when they were injured and simply needed prayer.

As my pro ball career came to an end, I recognized that I didn't have to try to be relevant to my teammates. As I remained reverent to God, I became the most relevant guy on the team when they needed help the most. To this day, I still receive messages from former players thanking me for talking with them and pointing them to Jesus. I don't claim my life was perfect by any stretch, but God showed me how relevant I could become by simply remaining reverent to Him.

> I will lift up my eyes to the mountains;
> From where shall my help come?
> My help comes from the LORD,
> Who made heaven and earth.
>
> —PSALM 121:1–2

INHERITANCE BEFORE INFLUENCE

To illustrate further, let's compare Daniel to Abraham's nephew, Lot, whose story is told in part in Genesis 19. Both of them achieved positions of great influence in their respective decadent cities—Daniel in Babylon and Lot in Sodom—but how they obtained their positions and what they did with them differed greatly.

As a leader in Sodom with a position of influence, Lot failed to impact his city's culture—in fact, he nearly lost his family to the pagans when he tried to appease them by offering his daughters to a sexually aggressive mob (v. 8). Talk about the fear of man leading your decisions! God said He would spare the city if He found ten righteous men, yet they didn't exist (Genesis 18:32). Lot chose to appease the crowd instead of appeal to God—to be relevant rather than reverent. As a result, he failed to influence his city, though he saved himself.

Lot stands as an example of what a righteous man looks like when he gives way before the wicked while trying to be relevant. He was spared from judgment but had zero influence over the culture of his city.

> Like a trampled spring and a polluted well
> Is a righteous man who gives way before the wicked.
> —PROVERBS 25:26

An interesting side note about the story of Lot: as he and his family were departing Sodom, his wife looked back toward the city and became a pillar of salt (Genesis 19:26). She became in her death what she and her husband should have been in their lives to the city—salt and light, which is what Christ commands all believers to be (Matthew 5:13–16).

Daniel, on the other hand, was a leader in Babylon and remained faithful to his convictions, no matter what the angry mob tried to do to him. The result was, once again, a testimony to the living God given to the culture of Babylon. As King Darius proclaimed, "I make a decree that in all the dominion of my kingdom men are to fear and tremble before the God of Daniel" (Daniel 6:26).

 A position of influence with man will never compare with the pathway to inheritance with God.

Jesus took reverence to His Father so seriously that He even called His own friend (Peter) "Satan" when he opposed God's plan (Matthew 16:23). That's intense! Jesus suffered as a righteous man, not deserving any kind of punishment, because He revered God even more than His natural desires. But in the end, the result was resurrection, exaltation, and salvation.

We should follow Christ's example as He delighted in the fear of the Lord.

Hurting people are looking for answers. And they don't need Christians to tell them what they *want* to hear—wrapping God and His Word around their personal agendas. They need Christians to tell them what they *need* to hear—the truth of God's Word that saves and sets free.

God has called us to speak the truth and meet people's *real* needs, just as Jesus and Daniel did. But we cannot do this unless our reverence for God outweighs our desire to be relevant. Then we will see the truth set people free. Just as Noah's ark brought life and salvation to his entire family, our reverence to God will bring the same to those around us.

TRANSFORMATION OR TRADITION

Remember, however, that the prophets warned us against counterfeit reverence. In our desire to fear God more than people, we must be careful not to fall into the trap of religious tradition.

> This people draw near with their words
> And honor Me with their lip service,
> But they remove their hearts far from Me,
> And their *reverence* for Me consists of tradition
>   learned by rote.
>
> —Isaiah 29:13

Read that verse carefully. The people of Judah developed a form of reverence that had outward piety without inward substance. In other words, they had religious devotion without hearts of reverence. They were not motivated by the internal conviction of honoring God. Their hearts were not transformed by a genuine, deep admiration and respect for God. They only repeated their routines—just the same old "Sunday service and midweek Bible study." Their relationship had become nothing more than religious activity. And they even thought their religion pleased God and gave them an escape from judgment.

By contrast, Daniel was a transformed man of conviction whose reverence set the stage for one of the most incredibly relevant lives a man has ever lived, even to this day. If you want to experience the same kind of conviction—conviction that transforms your heart—you must choose every day to live reverently in the fear of God—*your* God. He is the only One worth considering when the pressures of the culture demand that we simply blend in and be relevant.

How about you?

Transformation or tradition?

Relationship or routine?

Reverence or relevance?

Are you ready to make some life-changing choices?

As we move forward in these pages together, we want to encourage you to move deeper into your relationship with Christ. To prioritize reverence to God and not relevance to culture. To live with the same conviction as Daniel—and then to build commitments around those convictions so you will live courageously in today's Babylon.

PART II

COMMITMENT THAT TRANSFORMS MY LIFESTYLE

IN PART ONE, WE discussed the conviction that transformed Daniel's heart. His relationship with God, his identity, his worldview, and his reverence provided the deep, personal substructure for his daily life in Babylon.

Part two focuses on Daniel's daily life. His commitments were practical habits that transformed his lifestyle. Though ripped from his homeland and replanted in a pagan culture, he translated his original faith into godly customs. Thus, God's kingdom had a visible testimony in Babylon.

Daniel's *conviction* was his internal reservoir of strength. His *commitments* created a tangible conduit for that reservoir to flow into real life. That's how he was able to resist Babylon's influence and transform its culture. As we develop the same commitments, we will reap the same results.

Here are Daniel's commitments that transformed his lifestyle:

Draw the Line
Live with Excellence
Read God's Word
The Power of Prayer
The Strength of Humility
The Power of Purity

CHAPTER 6

DRAW THE LINE

The lines have fallen to me in pleasant places;
Indeed, my heritage is beautiful to me.

—Psalm 16:6

 God's blessings are only found within God's boundaries. Remove the boundaries and the blessings are replaced with burdens.

GROWING UP IN A tiny church where our dad was the preacher meant we not only heard him preach every Sunday but also heard him sing. Yeah, he led worship for a good part of his preaching career—and it was brutal. (Sorry, Dad.) But while his voice may not have been all that good, we know God was pleased with the words coming out of his mouth and with the heart with which he sang them.

One of Dad's favorite songs was "I Have Decided to Follow Jesus." Almost every Sunday we sang that song with the classic words:

I have decided to follow Jesus;
No turning back, no turning back.
The world behind me, the cross before me;
No turning back, no turning back.
Though none go with me, still I will follow;
No turning back, no turning back.[1]

As with so many of the great hymns, there is an amazing story behind this song. A family in the Indian province of Assam—a husband and wife, along with their two children—had professed faith in Christ and were baptized by a Welsh missionary in the 1880s. They then suffered intense persecution. The village leaders decided to make an example out of the family. Arresting them, they demanded the father renounce Christ. He responded by saying, "I have decided to follow Jesus, and there is no turning back."

They then killed his two children right in front of him. He responded to their martyring with these words: "The world can be behind me, but the cross is still before me." He would not deny Jesus. Again, they demanded he renounce his new faith. When once again he refused, they killed his wife. He then said, "Though no one is here to go with me, still I will follow Jesus."

The village leaders then killed him as well.

Within days of coming to Christ and within moments of one another's deaths, the entire family was ushered into the presence of the One from whom there was no turning back.

According to the Welsh missionary, when he returned to this village, a revival had broken out. Those who had murdered the family had themselves come to faith. He passed these reports along to the famous Indian evangelist Sandhu Sundar Singh, who made the brave man's dying words into the timeless hymn.[2]

What an amazing testimony! Nothing was going to deter this faithful man from the commitment he made to Jesus—nothing. That Indian brother dedicated himself to Jesus, and he followed through with practical action, costing him his life. Remember the next time you hear or sing this song, its words inspire us to deep commitment, even unto death.

DEPTH BY DISCIPLINES

Commitment takes place in two phases. The first phase is the commitment we make to God, pledging our whole hearts and promising to serve Him forever. Many Christians are crippled in their spiritual lives because of halfhearted commitments, and as such, they don't experience the peace and power of the Christian life.

The second phase is the practical steps we take that transform our lifestyles so we can live out the commitments we have made. Quite often the problem with uncommitted Christians is that their *internal convictions* are not cemented by *external commitments*—they've never made the practical commitments that transform the way they live.

A classic example of this is a Christian who can't remember the last time he actually read the Bible. If we truly make a wholehearted commitment to the Lord, this will manifest itself in commitments that help us grow close to Him.

To be transformers for God in the world, our internal convictions must be cemented by external commitments.

Years ago we both felt convicted by the Lord to wake up early and spend time with God before we began our day. But this kind of commitment would have been impossible if we hadn't made several other commitments first, such as getting to bed before 11:00 p.m., exercising regularly, eating healthy, and not watching TV before bed. If we stayed up late to watch a movie with the kids while wolfing down a bowl of ice cream, we could guarantee that a 5:00 a.m. wake-up time would turn into 7:00 a.m. (*Jason: For David, it's more like 9:00!*)

This is just one simple way we lived out our conviction early on. The overall idea is that we commit ourselves fully to God and then develop corresponding disciplines so we can fulfill that commitment.

ALL IN—100 PERCENT

Our purpose for this section of the book is to identify the commitments Daniel made that expressed his conviction and to encourage you to build these disciplines into your lifestyle. Total commitment to Christ cannot be built on the day of crisis. This process begins with our initial surrender and then is developed over time. We can only do this by God's grace, receiving power from His presence in prayer and His Word (more on this later). A committed lifestyle takes discipline to build. We can't just sit back and expect it to miraculously materialize.

Daniel and his friends built a destiny by committing to God long before they needed the courage to stand. Every day we determine to live committed lives, the better prepared we will be to live among lions when our own day in the den comes. Just before he got thrown to the beasts, six simple words reveal the depth of Daniel's commitment. Check them out in the following context:

> Now when Daniel knew that the document was signed, he entered his house (now in his roof chamber he had windows open toward Jerusalem); and he continued kneeling on his knees three times a day, praying and giving thanks before his God, *as he had been doing previously.*
>
> —DANIEL 6:10

"As he had been doing previously." There you have it— Daniel's dedication in full effect. He was 100 percent into serving God and obeying Him. His conviction worked its way into practical commitments that became the custom of his life and provided him with the courage he needed to face the lions.

Jesus displayed this same level of consistency with His commitments when He walked the earth. The same type of statement is used to describe Him in the verses that follow:

> He left that place and went to the region of Judea and beyond the Jordan. And crowds again gathered around him; and, *as was his custom,* he again taught them. (Mark 10:1 NRSV)

Jesus was committed to sharing the truth with others.

> When he came to Nazareth, where he had been brought up, he went to the synagogue on the sabbath day, *as was his custom.* (Luke 4:16 NRSV)

Jesus was committed to honoring the Sabbath.

> He came out and went, *as was his custom,* to the Mount of Olives; and the disciples followed him. (Luke 22:39 NRSV)

Jesus was committed to spending time alone with His Father.

Like Jesus, Daniel was all in. As a result, he stood when others bowed. He spoke when others were silent. He moved forward when others retreated—all because he built customs into his life, commitments to God that revealed his conviction.

STAYING INBOUNDS

In Daniel's lifestyle, we see him modeling five disciplines that we will discuss in the next several chapters:

1. Excellence
2. God's Word
3. Prayer
4. Humility
5. Purity

But here's the key: in order to develop those disciplines *in* his life, Daniel had to first embrace God's boundaries *around* his life. Those boundaries formed the framework on which Daniel built his life and established God's kingdom in Babylon. Without definite borders around his lifestyle, he may have wandered into spiritual territory that did not belong to him—places where God would not bless his works. But *within* those boundaries, Daniel knew God would bless what was built.

So Daniel joyfully embraced God's boundaries. He refused to wander wherever he wanted or draw his own borders. Rather, he allowed *God* to draw the lines, trusting those were best for him.

The same applies to us. We cannot talk about developing commitments unless we first have a healthy concept of God's boundaries. But this is a dangerous topic to discuss today. Talking about God's *blessings* is cool while talking about God's *boundaries* is uncool—even considered legalistic by some.

 What God has done for us is easy to talk about, but what God requires of us is more challenging to discuss.

God requires obedience to the clear-cut boundaries outlined in His Word. The first time we see this in Daniel's life is when he chose to submit to God's dietary boundaries as a young man in the king's court (Daniel 1). When he was offered the king's royal food, he instantly said no and set a practical plan into place for his friends' and his meals: "Please test your servants for ten days, and let us be given some vegetables to eat and water to drink" (v. 12). That's pretty cool—a young kid showing us what commitment looks like. We're sure the food probably looked and smelled amazing, as good as any Thanksgiving feast we've ever seen.

Four words describe exactly how Daniel turned his convictions into commitments: "But Daniel *made up his mind* that he would not defile himself with the king's choice food or with the wine" (v. 8).

This all starts with *making up our minds* to obey God by staying within the boundaries He sets for our lives. Daniel's lines were God's lines. God's lines were Daniel's lines.

 Daniel was committed to living within the boundaries because he was surrendered to the Boundary Giver.

And just to remind you, many theologians agree that because Daniel and his friends are described as "youths," they were not more than twenty years old and may have been much younger—in today's description, high school to college age.[3] Let that sink in.

We recognize Daniel's dietary boundaries do not apply to everyone today. God had set specific laws for ethnic Israel to differentiate them from the rest of the world, like not eating pork or meat with blood in it. These rules gave the Jews an opportunity to obey God—to be fully committed to Him. As weird as some of them may seem to us today, He established these boundaries so His people would stand out from the rest of the world—like chocolate chips in cookie dough.

In his book *To Be a Jew*, Rabbi Hayim Halevy Donin sums up dietary laws:

> The only hint or clue that the Biblical text itself provides as to the reason for all these regulations is that in almost every instance where the food laws are referred to in the Torah, we find a call to holiness. In Leviticus, Chapter 11, for instance,

following the entire section which lists what may and may not be eaten, the chapter concludes: "For I am the Lord your God; sanctify yourselves and be holy, for I am holy."[4]

This was the heart of Daniel's commitment. He desired to obey God and was not going to cross His line. As a result, he and his friends shined among their peers and received the Lord's favor. They weren't crippled in their spiritual lives as so many were then and are today. Instead, they thrived, running full speed in the power of God. "So you shall keep My statutes and My judgments, by which a man may live if he does them; I am the Lord" (Leviticus 18:5).

 God's boundary lines are in place for our protection. The Enemy tells us these are unnecessary restrictions keeping us from having fun when they are actually necessary restraints keeping us from being harmed.

Though in this life we will have trials and tribulations, when we make up our minds to truly commit our lives to God and obey Him fully, He makes up His mind to grant us favor and power in the midst of them all. Oswald Chambers wrote in *My Utmost for His Highest*, "When we choose deliberately to obey Him, then He will tax the remotest star and the last grain of sand to assist us with all His almighty power."[5] That's just plain incredible.

Take a look at the results of Daniel and his friends' commitment to God's dietary boundaries: "At the end of ten days their appearance seemed better and they were fatter than all the youths who had been eating the king's choice food. So the overseer continued to withhold their choice food and the wine they were to drink, and kept giving them vegetables" (Daniel 1:15–16).

LIFE LINES

Our parents taught us the value of boundaries early in life. They had to do this because we never stopped moving, which put us in constant danger.

When we were four, our family moved to Garland, Texas, to start a church. The first day we arrived, Dad stood in the driveway and looked around for a minute, and then he grabbed our hands and took us for a walk. He was going to set up boundaries for his two "Labrador puppies," as he often called us. He wanted to protect us.

We walked past the first house on the right, but just before getting to the second house, Dad stopped and said, "Boys, do you see this line in the sidewalk? That's your boundary line. Don't cross it." Then we walked the opposite way, two houses down on the other side. He said the same thing: "See *this* line in the sidewalk? That's your boundary line. Don't cross it."

As we walked home, he said, "Now you know the lines I've drawn for you to stay inside. You boys can play anywhere you want within those lines, but as soon as you cross them, you'll have to be disciplined."

Dad had drawn the lines—his boundaries for us. And it was our responsibility to stay within them. In time, we discovered the only way we would submit to staying within those lines was to surrender to the line-drawer—Dad. If we were not fully committed to obeying him, then his boundaries meant nothing. Fortunately for us, he believed in swift punishment, so we learned the lesson pretty fast.

We discovered very quickly there was freedom and safety within boundaries. So long as we stayed within our clearly defined limits, we could play as hard as we wanted without any fear. We lived full lives and thrived inside his lines of protection. Once we learned to stop focusing on where we *weren't* allowed to go, we had a blast within the area where we *were* free to go. Perspective is important when learning to live inside boundaries.

We also grew up in a time when weekend sports started to become popular—specifically, playing on Sunday. Today it's the norm, but back in our day the craze was new. Dad told us we weren't going to play organized sports on the day we set aside for the Lord. We initially bucked against this boundary, but in time we settled down and embraced it.

This wasn't a religious thing for Dad—as if he were going to get in trouble with God for letting us play. But he gave us this boundary to teach us to worship God and not sports. The way to learn that lesson was by denying ourselves one day a week. By God's grace, we learned this one well and came to love our day of rest.

Dr. James Dobson tells the story of how, in the early days of progressive education, the decision was made to remove the chain-link fence that surrounded a preschool playground. The educator theorized that children would feel more freedom if there were no boundaries around them. But to the contrary, when the fence was removed, all the boys and girls stayed closer together, playing only near the center of the area. Not only did they not venture out; they wouldn't even go *near* the boundary where the fence had been originally. The elimination of a physical boundary only restricted freedom.[6]

The same is true for adults. Imagine walking into a high-rise condo on the fiftieth floor and opening the door that leads out to the balcony. You then discover there is no railing. Would you feel safe stepping out on to the balcony? Not a chance! If you're anything like us and afraid of heights, you'd be scared to death to walk out there. But as soon as the railing goes up, you're free once again to enjoy the balcony.

Boundaries bring three very important things:

1. Freedom

    Inside our boundaries we find safety and certainty—blessings, not burdens. Like the train that finds both its clearest path and fastest speed only on the tracks, so we find our lives inside God's clearly drawn lines.

    > The lines have fallen to me in pleasant places;
    > Indeed, my heritage is beautiful to me.
    >
    > —PSALM 16:6

2. Framework

    Like the fence on the playground or the railing on the balcony, boundaries provide a clear-cut framework in which we may be free to pursue the powerful life to which God has called us.

    > You have ordained Your precepts,
    > That we should keep them diligently.
    > Oh that my ways may be established

To keep Your statutes!
Then I shall not be ashamed
When I look upon all Your commandments.
　　　　　　　　　　　　—PSALM 119:4–6

3. Fruit

Like a well-protected and well-managed garden, our lives cultivated within God's boundaries will thrive and glorify God by producing life in others. After all, fruit is not for the tree to enjoy, but for those who pick from its branches.

Walk as children of Light (for the fruit of the Light consists in all goodness and righteousness and truth).
　　　　　　　　　　　　—EPHESIANS 5:8–9

Today, many people demand there be no boundaries because they have rejected any thought of a Boundary Giver. But if we want to bring freedom, framework, and fruit to our hearts, homes, and culture, we must commit to Him and submit to His boundaries.

THE CROSS BEFORE US, THE WORLD BEHIND US

Commitment is an action we take in response to God. When we're committed to Him, this means there's no turning back. There's no halfway. Jesus went all the way with the cross, so we must do the same in taking up ours. In this daily sacrifice, His boundaries have become our boundaries.

If we want to live like Daniel, with the power to transform our world, then it's time to fully commit to God. But let's not stop there—let's build commitments into our lives that will drive us toward our destiny of bringing God glory on the earth.

Imagine the Indian martyr standing in front of you right now, his family with him. He takes out a sword and draws a line in the sand between him and you. Then he says, "All right, decision time. Are you going to commit? Join me over here if you're ready to go all in. Life won't always be easy, and hard times will come, but will you decide to follow Jesus?"

We're joining him and Daniel and all the committed of Christ. So let's step across the line and walk together as we follow Jesus. No turning back . . . no turning back.

CHAPTER 7

LIVE WITH EXCELLENCE

Then this Daniel became distinguished above all the other high officials and satraps, because an excellent spirit was in him. And the king planned to set him over the whole kingdom.

—Daniel 6:3 esv

 The favor of God gets you in the door, but excellence keeps you there.

FRESH OUT OF PRO baseball as newbie real estate agents, we didn't have much business coming in the door. So we'd show up to the office early in the morning, before anyone else, and hit our knees in prayer—right in front of the sales board where all the activity from the other agents was displayed. At this point, our names were nowhere to be found.

At sales meetings the other agents would talk about their business deals and how busy they were, yet it was nothing but crickets for us. At the time we had five kids between the two of us, so we were getting desperate. We *had* to get our business off the ground.

We'd bow in prayer every morning and lift our hands toward heaven, begging God to open doors and put His favor on our lives. We had studied the life of Daniel and recognized that excellence was one of the commitments that transformed his world, so we committed to do the same. We had made up our minds—no matter what God brought our way, we would act with excellence. Now we just needed God to open a door.

After several weeks of prayer and countless hours on the phone, the big break came with one call.

"Guys, I'm with a bank based in Dallas, Texas. I'm flipping through the Yellow Pages, looking for someone willing to sell a few dumpy foreclosure houses for us in your area. They're not worth much, and the first five companies I called declined, so I'm desperate."

Ha! He had no clue how desperate *we* were.

"We'll sell them! Where are they?" we asked. He interjected, "Hold on. Before you do that, drive by them, and let me know if you really want to do this. These houses are small and in bad shape."

"It's okay—your call is an answer to our prayers. We'll sell them for you, no matter what!" He was *not* expecting that. And to say we had an adrenaline rush is putting it lightly. God had just opened the door. We knew this was from Him.

After giving us the addresses, he faxed all the requirements to us to sell these homes for his bank. (Yes, we said fax. This was 2003.) At this point we read a key piece of information: the average time to inspect a house and provide all the initial services was seven days. As soon as we saw that, we knew this was our opportunity to exceed expectations. We had made a commitment to God that if He opened the door, we were going to be excellent and knock it out of the park for His glory. Seven days was not an option. We were going to do this in two.

Within a few hours of the banker's initial call, we had gone out to all the properties, changed the locks, taken pictures, and provided an analysis of the market value for each house. Although we had *no* idea what we were doing at the time, we were committed to excellence. That was the goal that guided us.

Arriving back at the office, we faxed all the information back to him. Within a few minutes, our phone rang. It was the banker saying, "Are you kidding me?! In all my years in this business, I've never seen this before. What you boys just did in a couple of hours normally takes agents several days. Do you think you can keep this up?"

In that moment we heard Rocky Balboa's bell! You know, the part in all his movies when he's on the ropes about to go down, then he hears the bell ring in his mind—the one where he knows he can fight and is going to do whatever it takes to win. Yeah, we heard *that* bell.

We responded, "If you send us everything you've got in our area, we guarantee to keep this same level of excellence all the way through the entire transaction."

Six months later we had sold nineteen houses for him *and* landed at the top of the sales board. Seven years later we had a hundred offices in thirty-five states. In 2010, we honored the banker and his wife publicly at our annual franchise conference in Charlotte. It was so awesome to have him sit in the audience as we gave our testimony about the way God used him to answer the prayer of two desperate brothers.

When excellence becomes a commitment that transforms your lifestyle, this opens the door for God to receive glory. He determines who, what, and where you serve; you just have to stay faithfully committed to serving with excellence.

Commitment to excellence is a primary expression of our conviction. As we said at the beginning of the chapter, the favor of God gets you in the door, but excellence keeps you there.

STEP INTO YOUR STADIUM

Excellence does not mean we have to be the best in the world. We just have to be *our* best right where God has placed us. This is how Daniel lived his life. He didn't try to defeat the people around him just so he could get ahead. He did his job with utmost excellence, and God took care of the rest. The same is true for us.

Faithfulness in what God has called you to do, right where He's called you to be, is the foundation for excellence.

We are *huge* college football fans. There is something really special about a packed stadium. We love hearing the pounding drums and screaming students and watching the schools go to war on the gridiron. Since we were kids, we wanted to see Notre Dame play Michigan in South Bend, Indiana—one of the oldest rivalries in college football history.

One day a good buddy and former player offered us tickets

to this legendary game. So we loaded up our boys and headed to South Bend. We hit the pep rally, took a tour of the locker room, ate tailgate food until we felt we were going to pop, and then walked into Notre Dame Stadium and took in the game. What a memorable weekend for us as dads, just getting to hang with our sons and "bro it out" for a few days.

But the most memorable part of the entire trip was not the game, the nostalgia, or even all the barbecue we shoved down our pieholes. Our unforgettable moment happened the night before the game. We attended an event where Lou Holtz, head coach of Notre Dame from 1986 to 1996, was the keynote speaker. In 1988, Holtz led his team to a perfect season, winning the Fiesta Bowl and the national championship.[1] He shared stories of former players and behind-the-scenes details on the road to becoming a champion. They may as well have played the theme song from *Rudy* because we all were ready to jump out of our seats! Holtz is a riveting speaker.

But Holtz said one thing that night we will never forget. He said he always gave one piece of encouragement to his team before a big game, telling them, "You don't have to be the best team in the *country*—you just have to be the best team in the *stadium*."[2]

That profound statement clicked in our hearts, turning on a whole new light. Be your best—in whatever stadium you're in. God has put each one of us in our own "stadium" with a specific set of talents and abilities designed for the task He wants us to accomplish. Each of us is one player with a position on His team. But He doesn't ask us to be the best in the *country* at something—He just asks us to be the best in our stadium, living faithfully right where He has placed us.

COMMITMENT THAT TRANSFORMS MY LIFESTYLE

PUT ME IN, COACH!

Okay, here comes another sports analogy applied to the first chapter of Daniel. This shows us the base paths of excellence:

First Base: "But Daniel made up his mind." (v. 8)

Second Base: "Now God granted Daniel favor." (v. 9)

Third Base: "So they entered the king's personal service." (v. 19)

Home Plate: They were "ten times better" than the others. (v. 20)

We must first make up our minds to commit ourselves to excellence. He then grants us favor and chooses the stadium where we will play our game. When we are excellent (*our* best) right where God puts us, He receives the glory, which means we've hit a walk-off home run! (*David: Jason didn't do that in baseball as often as I did.*)

Daniel's stadium was in the king's court in Babylon.

But most of us common folks never serve in the "king's court." And trying to be ten times better than the others? That's pretty impressive. Let's be real. This sounds out of reach for most of us normal people with normal jobs. Can *we* still hit home runs for God?

Of course! The good news is God doesn't call us to *be* Daniel. He only asks us to *learn* from Daniel's life so we can transform our world right where He's placed us—in our stadium. We just need to make up our minds to live a life of excellence for His glory.

Excellence is not a destination but a destiny—
being all that God designed us to be for His glory.

God called Daniel and his friends to be in places and do things that we may never experience. He equipped them with the tools necessary for their stadium. And He gave them the authority to do their jobs and the power to accomplish them with excellence. But we can do the same right where we are.

> Do you see a man skilled in his work?
> He will stand before kings;
> He will not stand before obscure men.
> —Proverbs 22:29

When we serve with excellence, God puts us in the presence of kings, or people of influence, promoting us as He wills. But we must remember—God doesn't call us to be *the* best but only to give *our* best.

HE NAILED IT!

Daniel and his friends achieved great influence in Babylon as a result of their excellent spirits. But influence wasn't their goal; rather, it was the by-product of achieving their goal of excellence.

Faithfulness leads to excellence, which opens
the door for influence.

During Jesus' early ministry, people from His hometown recognized Him as "the carpenter's son" (Matthew 13:55). On the surface this seems to be a generic statement about what he previously did for a living. But peeling back the layers, we realize a deeper truth to this label. The Greek word used for "carpenter"—*tektón*—means that Jesus was a skilled craftsman, versatile in His trade, which would have made Him an important part of the village economy. He wasn't just another carpenter hammering nails, doing the minimum to pay the bills. He was a master craftsman in woodwork.[3]

Jesus was a first-rate, paradigm-shifting carpenter, a master at His trade. Can you imagine if He had been a corner-cutting, compromise-making slob? This would have devalued His word with creditors and had customers chasing Him around town. At the very least, they would have been giving bad reviews, exposing His hypocrisy during His ministry. But this, of course, was not the case.

Whether hammering or healing, Jesus served with excellence.

When we first went into business, we were strongly cautioned not to put the Christian fish symbol on our business cards. We didn't realize this at the time, but some people in business had given Christians a bad name—their words didn't match their work. Instead of bringing glory to God, they brought shame to Christians in business.

Though we were willing to live with that stigma, we still chose not to put Christian symbols on any of our marketing material. We wanted our excellence to open the door for influence rather than mere symbols of our faith. Work well, and then your witness will work.

At age twenty-nine, Jesus wasn't sitting around, sipping

coffee, and thinking about how He could gain influence to set the stage for His future ministry. He was working with excellence as a carpenter right where God put Him. He was worshipping His Father through His work.

Work and worship go hand in hand. Work existed before sin entered the picture (Genesis 2:15) and is one of man's ways of worshipping God.

Daniel's work was worship. Jesus' work was worship. And both of them were excellent, which opened the door for influence to glorify the Father.

Here's a simple breakdown of the value of excellent work:

1. The *requirement* for excellent work is faithfulness.
2. The *reward* for excellent work is rest.
3. The *result* of excellent work is God receives the glory.

Jesus said, "I glorified You on the earth, having accomplished the work which You have given Me to do" (John 17:4). The earth is already filled with His glory, so when we work with excellence, this makes His glory visible to others—a reflection of His kingdom on the earth.

We all have a work to accomplish. Sometimes it's glamorous but usually not. I (David) remember leaving baseball and trading in my baseball bat for a broomstick as a janitor, yet I was convicted to serve God by sweeping floors with excellence in the same way I swung my bat. You may be a stay-at-home mom who had a dream to influence the world one day, but at the moment, you're changing diapers. Well, you *are* influencing the world—one spotless baby bum at a time! So, no matter what you do, be excellent right where you are—and God will be glorified, no matter how *stinky* the job is! (*David: That was actually Jason's line. I would not have said that.*)

ATTRACT, NOT DETRACT

"When a man's ways are pleasing to the LORD, He makes even his enemies to be at peace with him" (Proverbs 16:7). This verse has been a staple of ours since we started reading the Bible as kids. The way we live and act should help, not hinder, glorifying God in the earth. If Daniel were alive today, he would tip well, be kind to the Uber driver, deliver excellent service to his boss or his clients, put others first, and lead with value in his relationships—at home, at work, and in his community. He would be a giver, not a taker. He would not demand that people accept or possess his values, but would show the vitality of his value system in everyday life. He would be a fountain, not a drain.

In Babylon, Daniel's ways were so pleasing to the king that he found himself in the highest position of authority in the land. Even when Babylon was conquered and Darius the Mede became king, Daniel was promoted because of his excellence (Daniel 6:3). Yet living with this commitment doesn't always mean people are going to love and accept you.

Certain leaders hated Daniel. Their jealousy drove them to bring him down, so they looked for ways to accuse him. But "they could find no ground of accusation or evidence of corruption, inasmuch as he was faithful, and no negligence or corruption was to be found in him" (v. 4). So they sought to accuse him based on his commitment to God's law. Much like many activist groups today, this was their target for attack. They said, "We will not find any ground of accusation against this Daniel unless we find it against him with regard to the law of his God" (v. 5).

The same ways of God that led to Daniel's promotion also led to his persecution. This felt true in our own lives when HGTV decided not to go forward with our show. We stated in many interviews on national television, "The same faithfulness to God that got us hired got us fired."

As we mentioned earlier, Proverbs 22:29 teaches when we are faithful in our *work*, we will "stand before kings." This is *promotion*. But Mark 13:9 teaches when we are faithful in our *walk*, "they will deliver you to the courts, and you will be flogged in the synagogues, and you will stand before governors and kings for My sake, as a testimony to them." This is *persecution*.

 Faithfulness in your work will lead to promotion while faithfulness in your walk will lead to persecution.

Whether we're promoted or persecuted (though we don't like to call it persecution in America—it's really only pressure right now), we must be committed to excellence. Daniel's spirit of excellence was a powerful testimony, clearly revealed in the way he lived. In the midst of a pagan culture, although many saw his life and glorified God, others saw his life and sought for his death.

These diametrically opposed responses to God's faithful people have been the same throughout history and still remain today. Why? Because we are to be light in the world (Matthew 5:14), and light exposes both good works and evil deeds.

Check out the function of light in both of these verses:

"Let your light shine before men in such a way that they may see your good works, and glorify your Father who is in heaven." (v. 16)

"For everyone who does evil hates the Light, and does not come to the Light for fear that his deeds will be exposed." (John 3:20)

Our job is to shine the light, not control anyone's responses. Like Daniel, when our works are exposed, everyone should be able to see they are *good* works. Yet, when the world's evil deeds are exposed, we should prepare to be hated.

Excellence glorifies God, which will come with a price, even if it promotes us. So we must be prepared. But this should never deter us from shining the light and being excellent in all we do.

YOU'RE PART OF HIS PLAN

As much as you might want to be *like* Daniel, God doesn't want you to *be* Daniel—He wants you to be you! Your testimony is part of His divine plan to shine light and overcome the darkness (Revelation 12:11). It's your turn to run your lap of the race in your own stadium today. You have to be excellent and give your best for God's glory.

Your stadium may change from time to time, as it did for Daniel and so many others. But as he remained committed to God, his favor continued to open doors where he could serve with excellence and bring God glory. In the last verses of Daniel's story, we see he was encouraged to go his way until the end—not anyone else's way, but *his* way—to be faithful to do what God called him to do right in the stadium where God put him: "But as for you, go *your way* to the end; then you will enter into rest and rise again for your allotted portion at the end of the age" (Daniel 12:13). So what is your stadium today? Are you committed to excellence there? To achieve it, consider the following:

+ Commit to your place, walking in the power of the Holy Spirit right where you are.
+ Claim His power to work in excellence through you.
+ Complete the work He has given you to do with excellence.

Excellence is one of the commitments that transforms our lives, which in turn will transform our world—just as Daniel transformed his. And when you live with commitment like that, you will find the courage you need when the lions of Babylon start prowling around.

CHAPTER 8

READ GOD'S WORD

*This book of the law shall not depart from your mouth, but
you shall meditate on it day and night, so that you may be
careful to do according to all that is written in it; for then you
will make your way prosperous, and then you will have success.*

—JOSHUA 1:8

The intensity of our light is directly proportional
to time spent in God's Word—it shouldn't stay
"this little light of mine" forever.

THOSE WHO TURN THEIR conviction to follow Jesus into a
disciplined life are known as *disciples*. The most distinct mark
of God's genuine disciples is their commitment to His Word.
And those committed to God's Word will be transformers.

Jesus said, "If you abide in my word, you are truly my
disciples" (John 8:31 ESV). True disciples make God's Word their
very life. They do not view the Bible as an outdated relic meant
only to gather dust on a coffee table. Rather, they recognize in

107

the Scriptures the sum and substance of Jesus Himself—the Word become flesh (John 1:1). A disciple doesn't just read the Word, but also studies, memorizes, meditates upon, and, overall, devours its pages. A disciple craves God's Word the way a hungry man longs for food. (*Jason: Or like our dad craves Fudgsicles!*)

Ultimately, and most important, a disciple *does* the Word of God—he or she knows that *learning* must lead to *living*. "Sustain me according to Your word, that I may live" (Psalm 119:116).

Those who seek to follow Daniel's example and transform their world will commit to God's Word with every ounce of their being as if their very lives depend on it.

The word *disciple* doesn't have the same meaning it once did back in Bible times. As a matter of fact, we've watered it down so much that very little of what we do today would be considered true biblical discipleship—especially when it comes to God's Word. For instance, did you know that most Jewish boys were expected to memorize the first five books of the Bible (the Torah) before their thirteenth birthday? (*Jason: I can feel a cold sweat coming on.*) Although not all of them accomplished this feat, for those who wanted to become disciples of a rabbi (teacher), memorization was mandatory. Once the boys memorized Genesis through Deuteronomy, they went on to the prophetic books—such as Isaiah, Jeremiah, and Ezekiel. They not only were supposed to know these books by memory but also had to understand their context and be able to explain the meanings when asked. The goal was not "I just need to know this for the test," but rather "I need to know this for my life."

A few years ago we listened to a series of lectures by Ray Vander Laan that was given at Focus on the Family, titled "Follow the Rabbi." Among other things, he discussed the elements of discipleship. By the time a Jewish boy was fourteen, a rabbi would grill him with questions about specific passages of Scripture. The boy was expected to know the exact references and be able to recite them and provide the verses before *and* after to establish context so he could explain what the passage meant. At age fourteen!

Each rabbi had disciples—young men with the goal of becoming just like him. For a Jewish boy to become a disciple of a renowned rabbi would be like one of our kids becoming an NBA or NFL star. This was a big deal.

Typically a boy would become a disciple between the ages of fourteen and sixteen, depending on his understanding of God's Word. Once he knew the Torah by memory and also the prophetic books, he would present himself to a rabbi and ask to be one of his disciples. The rabbi would then test the boy with a series of questions about the Scriptures to see if he really knew them. He was looking to see if this kid could become *just like him*, which was the goal of every rabbi for his disciples. If he felt confident he was able, he would then say, "Come follow me." This was a pass-or-fail test.

There was no greater honor in that day for a young Jewish teenager than to be told he could become *just like* the rabbi. But to be chosen, these young disciples had to know the Word of God from memory. (*David: Umm . . . is anyone feeling reproved like me right now?*) If the rabbi felt the boy didn't fully know and understand the Word of God, he would lovingly encourage him to go and work in a trade. He could still become godly and follow the Lord, but he could not be a disciple of the rabbi.[1]

Now *that's* how committed to God's Word true disciples were to be. But here's what we like best about this story: just when we feel almost worthless compared to these young boys, Jesus appears on the scene.

The Lord chose twelve guys who were all employed in common trades. He didn't get the top dogs who already knew God's Word like the back of their hands. Sure, the disciples knew Scripture, as most Jewish boys did, but they didn't know it like those who could become disciples of a rabbi.

Jesus picked the guys who failed the test. He chose the ones the world would consider the B team. Is there any wonder that these guys immediately dropped their nets and followed Him? They had been chosen by Rabbi Jesus, and He believed they could become *just like Him*.

 If we want the transformational life of Jesus to flow through us into our world, we cannot do it apart from a commitment to His Word.

But it doesn't stop there. Jesus Christ believes *we* can be just like Him. All those who are willing to surrender fully to Him can become His disciples. We cannot forget what this really means though—the connection between discipleship and knowing God's Word. As Christ asks us to follow Him, we should fully commit to knowing His Word so we "may be adequate, equipped for every good work" in our Babylon (2 Timothy 3:17).

THIS IS YOUR CAPTAIN SPEAKING

Have you ever wondered how airline pilots can accurately fly right through the middle of the clouds? This always baffled us until we heard a pilot explain how they are taught to fly the plane from the instrument panel—not from their own sight when looking through the windows. They have to use the instruments, not their own vision, to make sure the plane is positioned correctly and heading in the right direction.

There's no way Daniel could have navigated the clouds of Babylon without the help of his instrument panel—God's Word. Even in the midst of darkness, when he probably felt he was flying blind, Daniel positioned himself correctly and headed in the right direction. He understood God's plan for His people in Babylon because he sought God by reading the prophet Jeremiah: "I, Daniel, observed in the books the number of the years which was revealed as the word of the LORD to Jeremiah the prophet for the completion of the desolations of Jerusalem" (Daniel 9:2).

For Daniel, studying God's Word wasn't just a crisis intervention, a one-time event, or a religious routine to please a god who didn't care about him. He diligently sought the Lord through the Scriptures as a matter of practice and custom. Daniel knew God loved him and his people. That love was written into physical words on paper. He was a lifelong student of the Scriptures—as all true disciples are.

So why didn't Daniel try to resist the king of Babylon or, at least, gather some friends and try to escape back to Jerusalem? He knew from God's Word that such actions would fail. God said through the prophet Jeremiah that judgment was certain, Babylon would prevail, and any resistance to that plan would fail. Any "prophets" saying otherwise were *not* speaking for the Lord (Jeremiah 23:16). In fact, Daniel also knew God used Jeremiah to advise His people to settle in Babylon and make the best of their lives: "Build houses and live in them; and plant gardens and eat their produce. . . . Seek the welfare of the city where I have sent you into exile" (29:5, 7). (More on this later.)

Daniel trusted God's Word as his instrument panel rather than his own ideas and impulses. Though this may not have been popular wisdom or easy to hear, Daniel clung to Scripture when it said,

> If you will indeed stay in this land, then I will build you up and not tear you down, and I will plant you and not uproot you; for I will relent concerning the calamity that I have inflicted on you. Do not be afraid of the king of Babylon . . . for I am with you to save you and deliver you from his hand.
>
> —JEREMIAH 42:10–11

As he studied Scripture, Daniel fully understood that the Jews were to stay put right where God had placed them and that His Word clearly contradicted anyone trying to convince them otherwise. With this understanding of Scripture, Daniel didn't just survive—he thrived. He was able to navigate through the clouds as God's man in Babylon.

PASSION FOR THE PAGES

Dad told us when we were kids that if we read the Bible just five minutes every day, we'd still have twenty-three hours and fifty-five minutes left to do whatever we needed to do. He said that eventually our hearts and minds would transform to be like Christ's—if only we would commit to consistent time in His Word.

By the time we graduated from high school, five minutes was no longer enough time. We craved much more of God's Word. This commitment was the single best decision we ever made as Christians to transform our lives.

In the same way that people don't find precious jewels just sitting on the surface of the ground, we had to dig deep in the Word and spend time alone chiseling away before valuable nuggets of truth emerged. And once we started discovering, we couldn't stop digging. The more we read and meditated on His Word, the more we realized why Dad had spent so much time reading his Bible. Every morning, we'd see him either praying on his knees by the couch or sitting on his kitchen stool reading his Bible. So we began forming the habit of doing the same things each morning, not because we had a natural desire to wake up early, but because we knew this was best for us as disciples.

 Commit to consistent time in God's Word, and the motivation will follow. In time your heart will catch up with your habit.

God taught us that *action often precedes motivation*. We had to force ourselves to get out of bed, and eventually the motivation followed. The conviction was already there, but we needed the raw commitment to put it into action. Then, over time, our hearts caught up with our habit. We began to experience motivation to wake up and spend time with God in His Word. And the more time we spent with Him, the more we wanted to spend with Him. By the time our motivation finally kicked into gear, the habit had already been formed. *Boom!* More transformation.

We often tell kids, "Don't wait until you *want* to spend time with God. Just do it, and keep doing it until you want to do it—then you won't be able to live without your time in His Word."

SHOOTING DOWN THE LIES

Have you ever noticed of all the armor of God in Ephesians 6, the "sword of the Spirit," which is the Word of God, is the only offensive weapon? Here's the context:

> Therefore, put on every piece of God's armor so you will be able to resist the enemy in the time of evil. Then after the battle you will still be standing firm. Stand your ground, putting on the belt of truth and the body armor of God's righteousness. . . . Put on salvation as your helmet, and take the sword of the Spirit, which is the word of God.
>
> —EPHESIANS 6:13–14, 17 NLT

How are we supposed to fight the Enemy in the time of evil if we don't have a sword—our only offensive weapon? And the "belt of truth" holds the entire spiritual uniform together. If we don't have the belt—the truth as revealed in God's Word—we'll be fighting with our pants down around our ankles! Not a pretty sight.

Today many Christians refuse to buckle their belts and pick up their swords. As a result, the Enemy of our souls is robbing, killing, and destroying in our land. We act as if we are defenseless against him even though God has outfitted us with His own armor! We simply must choose to put on our suit and pick up our sword.

My (Jason's) wife was deathly afraid of having a gun in our house even though I explained to her that we are much safer having one than not. Her reasons for not wanting a gun were twofold: she had heard that others had used them improperly and bad stuff had happened, and she didn't know how to use one herself. But without a gun in the house, each time I went out of town, she was fearful because she felt unprotected. Her faith was replaced with fear because she lacked a proper weapon.

I figured the only way around this was to buy a gun and train her to use it. That makes sense, right? After several days of training, we discovered she's actually a sharpshooter! Now she's fully comfortable with a gun and prepared to use her weapon to protect our home when I'm gone. With the proper weapon in her hand and the ability to use it, she can now resist any enemies that might seek to harm our family. Her defenselessness turned to her potential for offensive action through proper knowledge and training.

In the same way, instead of using the sword of the Spirit to fight back, many Christians today are gripped by fear as they watch the Enemy attacking their homes and this country. They simply don't have God's weapon in their hands.

Just as my wife experienced fear because she didn't have a weapon and had misinformed reasons for not owning one, many Christians have yet to pick up their greatest weapon. Why? The Bible has been improperly applied in the past, and there is a lack of understanding of how to properly use it. We can't let this happen.

Our defenselessness must turn to offensive action through proper knowledge and training. We can't shrink back in fear. We must advance and stop retreating. We need to commit to learning Scripture so that when the Enemy comes prowling around, all we've got to do is let God's sword do the work. In those moments we simply have to pull out our weapon and use the truth to destroy the lie. The Enemy doesn't stand a chance against a disciple whose belt of truth is buckled and who is trained with the sword of the Spirit.

DISCERNING DIRECTION

One of the many benefits of studying God's Word is that He provides us with the ability to discern between good and evil. When Daniel's life was on the line the first time, he replied "with discretion and discernment to Arioch, the captain of the king's bodyguard, who had gone forth to slay the wise men of Babylon" (Daniel 2:14).

Years before Daniel entered the scene, we see this same type of discernment in King Solomon. We often emphasize how he asked for wisdom when God visited him. But he also asked for *discernment*. He wanted the ability to discern between good and evil so he could properly lead God's people: "Give Your servant an understanding heart to judge Your people to discern between good and evil. For who is able to judge this great people of Yours?" (1 Kings 3:9).

And God granted his request. Solomon first revealed his God-given discernment in an amazing way. He asked for a *sword* when two mothers were fighting over a baby. Since he couldn't discern who the real mother was, he made use of a weapon to make the distinction. Of course, he had no intention of ever hurting the child, but the moment the sword entered the picture, the truth came to light—the real mom was revealed and the imposter was exposed (1 Kings 3:16–28).

The sword of the Spirit makes a clear distinction between good and evil, right and wrong, truth and lies. We have grown ignorant of God's Word, and as a result, many adult Christians today are walking around much like infants, having no sense of right and wrong. As the writer of Hebrews warned:

> For everyone who partakes only of milk is not accustomed to the word of righteousness, for he is an infant. But solid food is for the mature, who because of practice have their senses trained to discern good and evil.
>
> —HEBREWS 5:13–14

 Without diligence in God's Word, there will be no discernment—and without discernment, there will be no sense of direction.

When God's Word is a closed book, the light of discernment is dimmed, and everything becomes a strange shade of gray.

Do you see this happening in today's culture?

We need discernment in the church more than ever. The only way this will come is when the sword of the Spirit is unsheathed and wielded in our lives, homes, churches, and communities. Like Daniel, we must study, know, and then act on the Word of God.

GOD'S WORD VERSUS OUR WORDS

We were once asked to speak at a theological seminary on a panel discussing Christian influence in society. We encountered some interesting dialogue among the panelists about how each of them approached the Bible.

A few of them who claimed to be Christians were far more liberal than we were in their approach to Scripture. When asked what their personal Bible studies looked like, each responded in similar fashion: "We just open the Bible and try to find *our own* truth." They were basically saying that they start with their own experience and then look to the Bible to support what they think.

I (David) was just about to speak when Jason grabbed the microphone and said, "There are only two ways to approach the Bible: start with *you*—where you take your beliefs and experience, then wrap the Bible around *them*. Or start with *God*—where you take the Bible, then wrap your beliefs and experience around *it*."

He continued, "If you approach reading the Bible with *you* as the starting point, then you can get God's Word to say almost anything you want, and you'll then justify any behavior you want. There's no such thing as your *own* truth."

He then added, "Biblical Christians start with God first and then allow our experiences to be interpreted through His Word as it tells us what we should believe—not the other way around. We submit to His Word. His Word does not submit to us. He *is* Truth."

You could've heard a pin drop. Some people in the crowd were beaming with delight while others just sat there in stunned silence.

Despite what our panelist friends believed, we must approach God's Word on *His* terms, not ours. He is the beginning, our starting point. He is the end—the One with the final say. He is Alpha *and* Omega, the first *and* last (Revelation 22:13).

Though our experiences certainly affect what we understand the Bible to say at different times in our lives, we cannot allow our own experiences to determine what God's Word says. This is at the root of humanistic (man-centered) Bible study. When reading God's Word, we either begin with God or begin with us. There is no middle ground. You're either worshipping God through Bible study or worshipping yourself. John R. W. Stott once said, "We must allow the Word of God to confront us, to disturb our security, to undermine our complacency and to overthrow our patterns of thought and behavior."[2] This is exactly what God-centered Scripture study will produce.

We should never mold what the Bible says to fit our own ends. Rather, we should allow the Bible to mold us. This is especially true for younger Christians who are new to the study of God's Word. Here are three examples of what they may say or be thinking:

> "It's easy to say that homosexuality is a sin until one of your
> kids comes back from college claiming he or she is one."
> "I know God hates divorce, but I also know He wants me to
> be happy."
> "I know a Christian isn't supposed to lie, but if I tell the
> truth now, I'll lose my business."

As difficult and challenging as life may get in all our personal relationships, we cannot let certain experiences or feelings be placed above the truth of Scripture.

Wrap your beliefs around the Bible. Never wrap
the Bible around your beliefs.

When spiritual leaders approach God's Word from a man-centered viewpoint where experience takes the lead, they often twist the words to make the text say things that aren't true. Those who use the Word in this way are the people of whom the apostle Paul warned the elders in Ephesus when he told them, "I know that after my departure savage wolves will come in among you, not sparing the flock; and from among your own selves men will arise, speaking perverse things, to draw away the disciples after them" (Acts 20:29–30).

But we must "defend Christian truth as God's instruments for transforming culture," as Chuck Colson said.[3]

FEED YOUR FAITH

Yes, sometimes Scripture can be tough to read, yet the complexity should be an invitation to dig deeper, to search for those hidden jewels worth more than gold. And you may not understand everything you read either. But so what? You might not understand how a black cow can eat green grass under a blue sky and produce white milk, but you don't pour water on your Wheaties because you don't understand how milk is produced.

When you read Scripture, you feed your spirit and grow supernaturally. Today is the day for you to make a renewed commitment to God's Word.

Do you own a Bible or have a Bible app, but find little to no time to open it? Take our dad's advice and start with reading five minutes a day. Whether for the first time or the first time in a long time, start a habit and let your heart follow. We'll make you a promise—the five minutes you commit to the Bible will begin to shape your other twenty-three hours and fifty-five minutes of the day.

Our world is starving for disciples who know God's Word and can apply its truth with laser-sharp precision to the issues people face. And one of the best parts about reading the Bible—it will put you on your knees and drive you to prayer.

CHAPTER 9

THE POWER OF PRAYER

The effective prayer of a righteous man can accomplish much.
—James 5:16

 Our goal is to become not only prayer warriors but warriors through prayer.

W E HAD THE PRIVILEGE of hearing Lysa TerKeurst's testimony at the 2015 K-LOVE Fan Awards in Nashville. She shared about how her two adopted sons from war-torn West Africa learned to pray.

Lysa said, "My boys lived as orphans in Liberia. Most days they didn't know where their next meal was coming from. They had no food to bring to school, so they had to sit separate from the kids who came from families that provided them with packed lunches. Their teachers feared the orphans would steal or beg for food from the other students. They were hungry always and afraid for their lives often. So when they prayed, they prayed *surviving* prayers, not *thriving* prayers."[1]

If you're like us, you probably have a difficult time recalling the last time you prayed a surviving prayer. To be honest, we've prayed countless thriving prayers—because we have so much opportunity in this country—but surviving prayers are few and far between.

For the most part, our physical situation in America has not gotten to the point of survival mode. But our spiritual condition has. We must start praying the same kind of prayer in spiritual matters as those boys prayed in physical ones—desperately asking God to transform our world.

What's amazing is that these orphan boys' surviving prayers turned into thriving situations as they were selected, along with ten other orphans, to sing in a chorus that traveled to the United States. As a result of that trip, both boys were adopted by the TerKeurst family. Today, they are American citizens with thriving families, and now they also pray thriving prayers. Their entire lives transformed!

Daniel prayed survival prayers with such fervency and power that he both transformed his world and even altered the heavens—literally. After three weeks of prayer, he received an angelic visitor, who said, "Do not be afraid, Daniel, for from the first day that you set your heart on understanding this and on humbling yourself before your God, your words were heard, and I have come in response to your words" (Daniel 10:12).

Now that's some effective praying!

Daniel and his friends also had to pray for physical survival when the king ordered they were to be killed along with all the wise men:

Then Daniel went to his house and informed his friends, Hananiah, Mishael and Azariah, about the matter, so that

they might request compassion from the God of heaven concerning this mystery, so that Daniel and his friends would not
be destroyed with the rest of the wise men of Babylon.

—DANIEL 2:17–19

And God delivered them by giving Daniel revelation—not
only of the king's dream but of world history and God's kingdom.
The interpretation revealed the rise and fall of nations succeed-
ing Babylon—Medo-Persia, Greece, and Rome—with God's
kingdom ultimately trumping them all and filling the earth. And
Daniel received the dream and its interpretation because he and
his friends sought hard after heaven in prayer.

God's answer did more than get these boys out of trouble; it
also transformed the entire situation and gave us a major prophecy
for the ages. Daniel's desperate prayer for physical survival literally saved the lives of many other wise men, launched Daniel into
a powerful prophetic ministry, and promoted both Daniel and his
friends into the highest ranks of the Babylonian administration.

We repeat: now *that's* some effective praying!

God can turn our surviving prayers into prayers of thriving.
But let's look deeper. Notice that once God blessed Daniel with
the answer, Daniel blessed God back:

> "Let the name of God be blessed forever and ever,
> For wisdom and power belong to Him.
> "It is He who changes the times and the epochs;
> He removes kings and establishes kings . . .
> "It is He who reveals the profound and hidden things . . .
> "To you, O God of my fathers, I give thanks and praise,
> For You have given me wisdom and power,

Even now You have made known to me what we
requested of You,
For You have made known to us the king's matter."
—Daniel 2: 20–23

Daniel didn't just petition God—he praised Him! Daniel's prayer life matured into more than a tool for survival; it became a celebration of God's greatness. This is the kind of prayer life that transforms the world. Even though we must pray for our needs, Daniel's example shows us that genuine prayer is not me-centered but *God-centered*.

A prayer life filled with praise opens the floodgates of deep friendship with God, connecting our hearts and making prayer an intimate bond rather than a religious exercise or a mere business transaction. Transformational prayer, then, must include our personal petitions but must soar beyond those into recognizing the awesomeness of God Himself.

 Powerful prayers are not centered on petitions but on praise.

Too often we limit our prayers to things we want, as if God were a spiritual vending machine, but fail to "pour out [our] heart[s] before Him" in high praise and intimate worship (Psalm 62:8). Above all, prayer should be first about God, not us. Think of the difference between a love letter and a to-do list. Which would you rather receive?

Over time, Daniel developed an active prayer life; he didn't wait until he was in trouble to pray. Prayer became a commitment that turned into habit. That habit then intertwined with his character. As with David (2 Samuel 7:18–29), prayer became part of Daniel's constitution as a human being. Even when the laws of the land singled him out and targeted his petitions (more on this in chapter 14), he never cowered in fear or hid his faith but stood strong. He could do nothing else.

Prayer transforms *everything*—our lives *and* the world around us. Elisabeth Elliot said, "Prayer lays hold of God's plan and becomes the link between His will and its accomplishment on earth."[2] People who pray as Daniel prayed merge heaven and earth in their souls. They become doorways for God's kingdom to enter Babylon. They don't just become prayer warriors but warriors through prayer.

Let's pray like this today! Let's lay hold of a renewed and dedicated commitment to coming before our heavenly Father, just as Daniel did.

DIVINE DIALOGUE

How did Daniel pray with power and authority? He first focused on the *person* of God and His *people*. Then he established the right *posture*, remained *patient*, and stayed *persistent* in prayer. (Sorry about all the alliteration—we've got Baptist roots!)

When Daniel prayed, he stood upon the two greatest commandments: love the Lord your God and love others as yourself (Matthew 22:37–39). This provides the foundation upon which we are to stand when we pray. It's all about the person of God and the people He's created.

The Person of God

Daniel saw prayer as a two-way street of communication between him and God—not a one-way "gimme fest" but a genuine conversation that connected him with his heavenly Father. He built specific times into his day to spend time with God and to connect intimately.

One of the customs we've had with our wives since we've been married is that *every* Friday night is date night. We don't *need* this time to be "married;" we need this time to cultivate intimacy—the one thing that relationships can't exist without.

On our date nights, what if we took our wives out and spent the entire evening talking about ourselves, what we want, what we think, and what we want our wives to do? How do you think this would go? How would they feel? Can you say, "*Not a good night*"?

We grow in intimacy with our wives during these dates because we have conversations with them—they talk, we listen; we talk, they listen. And the result of a two-way conversation like this is intimacy—true, genuine connection and acceptance are infused into our relationships. (How about a fist-bump for date night?)

 Prayer is a two-way conversation to connect and communicate with our Father. It's not about getting things from God—it's about getting to God and experiencing intimacy with Him.

In the same way, when we pray, we talk to God, but we also listen. This builds our intimacy with Him. Listening for Him to speak to us should be an important aspect of our prayer times.

We are to focus not on getting answers to our prayers but on growing with the God who answers them.

In his classic devotional *My Utmost for His Highest*, Oswald Chambers echoes this idea: "Spiritual lust makes me demand an answer from God instead of seeking God Who gives the answer. . . . Whenever the insistence is on the point that God answers prayer, we are off the track. The meaning of prayer is that we get hold of God, not of the answer."[3]

Prayer is about getting to know the God to whom we pray because we have a relationship with our Father. Approaching God with the focus on Him provides power when we pray and, more importantly, creates intimacy with our Father.

The People of God

God convicted me (Jason) about my prayer life in my mid-thirties. (I know. I'm getting old.) David and I had traveled to Dallas for business, and I woke up early one morning to spend time with the Lord. As I walked outside, I felt a real burden to pray the Lord's Prayer, as Jesus taught us to do, and to meditate on each word.

I got to the first word, "Our," and stopped. I felt the Spirit rush over me, as if He were saying, "See? It's not just about *you*."

So I began to pray that morning with the mind-set of "us" instead of "me." I realized I didn't just need to pray *for* people but *with* people—God's people. Even though I was alone at that moment, my heart was with my brothers and sisters in Christ. I was praying as the church. I lost myself in the body of Christ, yet I found myself there as well.

I wasn't concerned about *my* daily bread anymore but *our* daily bread—including those in third-world countries and around the world. Instead of just confessing my own sins, I confessed the sins of my nation and of God's people—as Daniel did when he prayed (Daniel 9:4–19).

My prayer life began to change that morning. When I ended the prayer with "for Yours is the *kingdom* and the *power* and the *glory* forever, amen," I felt a fresh surge of power like I had never experienced before. I put God's *kingdom*—not my own—at the center of my prayer; therefore, He infused me with His *power* to bring Him *glory*—in that order—kingdom, then power, then glory.

That day I realized the raw power of prayer with an *us* mindset. For God to pour out His mercy on our nation, we must be unified in prayer, in the Spirit, as a body of believers. Unified prayer is the key to heaven's kingdom, power, and glory coming to earth (Psalm 145:18; Proverbs 15:29; Matthew 7:11; Luke 18:1; Colossians 4:2).

Daniel modeled the *us* prayer when he identified himself with his Jewish brothers and sisters who had sinned before him. He prayed, "*we* have sinned . . . *we* have not listened . . . open shame belongs to *us* . . ." (Daniel 9:4–8) Many of the sins that brought judgment on his nation occurred before Daniel was even born. But he still bore their burden. He was more concerned about God's people than himself.

Some Christians today don't feel the weight of our sin as a church and a nation—as if they are outside looking in. They don't want to lump themselves into the sinful mix as Daniel did. We must confess that we, as God's children, have *all* sinned and are *all* in need of healing today.

One hallmark of the great revivals throughout history is the unified humility and prayer of God's people. They would gather together to confess their sins, repenting publicly and openly before God and one another. When the Spirit moves among a body of believers who identify themselves as "us" rather than "me," this releases God's power to transform the world. The Bible promises, "For where two or three have gathered together in My name, I am there in their midst" (Matthew 18:20).

POSTURE

The power of prayer is maximized only with the proper *posture* of prayer: we are to *keep watch* when we pray.

While the physical posture of prayer is certainly important— bowing or kneeling, as Daniel did three times a day (Daniel 6:10)—here we are referring to an internal disposition where we look and listen for God at all times in all things. This is keeping watch. Daniel was always watching for God, so he wasn't caught off guard when the angels showed up or even when the lions stalked.

Posture matters a great deal to God. For another example from the Bible, turn to the story of Gideon in Judges 7. The Lord had promised Gideon He would deliver Israel from the oppressive Midianites. So Gideon assembled an army, but God told him it was too big, and He devised a test to whittle the force down to size. When Gideon's army reached the river to drink, God told him to keep the men who used their hands to cup the water to their mouths, which were only three hundred. The rest, those who put their faces in the water, were asked to leave. We believe they were cut because they didn't keep watch. In a time of war you must keep your eyes up and watch for the enemy. We cannot afford to bury our heads in the water and be caught unaware when attack comes.

Courage without keeping watch disqualifies those who want to fight. Prayerless warriors don't get to fight. God's method of choosing the army with which Gideon would do battle was based on their ability to keep watch.

On the night Jesus was betrayed, He took Peter, James, and John with Him into the Garden of Gethsemane to prepare for His crucifixion (Matthew 26:40–45). He left them with a very clear instruction: "keep watch." They were to stay alert and keep their eyes open to avoid temptation when the Enemy came.

As Scripture tells us, they fell asleep. When Jesus found them sleeping, He woke them up and gave the command: "keep watching *and* praying." Yet they failed again.

Suddenly, they were startled awake again, but this time the enemies of Christ were already upon them. And the first thing Peter reached for was his sword, cutting off a man's ear (v. 51). Because Peter failed to keep watch and pray, he grabbed the wrong weapon when the enemy showed up. This is how important keeping the right posture in prayer can be; otherwise, we'll grab the wrong weapon when we're awakened. This often looks like anger or pride in the face of being reviled, returning evil for evil or insult for insult. We must not take matters into our own hands, as the old saying goes, but place the circumstance in God's as we keep watch.

Check this out:

- If you're *not* in the right posture of prayer by keeping watch, then:

1. You'll miss God when He shows up.
2. You'll grab the wrong weapon when the enemy shows up.

+ But if you are in the right posture of prayer by keeping watch, then:
   1. You're not surprised when God shows up.
   2. You're not surprised when the enemy shows up.

 Maintaining a disposition of expectancy will open our eyes and ears to see and hear God when others don't.

Our posture of prayer must consistently be one of keeping watch—always looking for God in all things, keeping our eyes up, scanning the horizon as the Enemy of our souls seeks to devour our homes, churches, and nation. This does not make us suspicious but simply keeps us alert. The best offense is the sneak attack, but when we're keeping watch, it's impossible for the Enemy to get the jump on us.

Eyes up, ears open, hearts bowed—this is the strategic and effective posture of prayer.

PATIENCE

Keeping watch in prayer requires a great deal of patience. Daniel displayed patience when he prayed, especially given the fact he knew he was going to be in Babylon for seventy years (Daniel 9:2).

As a devout Jew, Daniel had undoubtedly read Isaiah's writings and knew the reward for waiting patiently on the Lord:

> Yet those who wait for the LORD
> Will gain new strength;
> They will mount up with wings like eagles,
> They will run and not get tired,
> They will walk and not become weary.
>
> —ISAIAH 40:31

Our job is *not* to mount up with wings—our job is to wait on the Lord. The strength to walk, run, and even fly will come from God in His time.

We're two of the most impatient guys on the planet. Seriously. In 2008, we prayed and asked God about buying a piece of land for our new real estate office. We both felt God gave us His *yes*, but we didn't wait for any further instruction from Him—we didn't get His *go*. We had our wings spread, but there was no wind. So we just jumped out and made the purchase anyway. (The complete story is in our first book, *Whatever the Cost*.)

Two years later we realized this was the biggest business mistake we had ever made. To salvage the deal, we had to "flap our wings" as fast as we could just to keep everything together.

 If you don't wait for the Lord, you may still have wings—but more like a hummingbird, you work a lot harder and fly a lot lower.

Without patience in prayer that waits for God's wind, you'll end up exhausted, without His strength and power to accomplish

His work. All you have to do is spread your wings (fully trust in God for the results) while He does the work. Thriving prayers require patience and waiting on His wind to come.

Before you start flapping, wait patiently for God's favor.

PERSISTENCE

As we wait patiently in prayer, we must also remain persistent, no matter how weary we may become.

Daniel gave us a picture of how important persistence is. He prayed and fasted for three straight weeks—he didn't even focus on his hygiene during this time (Daniel 10:2–3). He was an absolute mess on the outside, but he was fully alive on the inside, and God spoke to him despite his exhaustion.

Twenty-one days later, Daniel got a response to his prayers. We repeat—twenty-one days later. That's a long time! What Daniel didn't realize was that on the first day he had begun to seek the Lord, an angel was sent to go to him, but the angel was detained in spiritual warfare the whole time (vv. 12–14).

What if Daniel had quit after five days, ten days, even twenty days? He might have missed out on one of the most amazing angelic visitations recorded in the Bible. But because his heart was set on seeking the Lord with persistence, God showed up in a big way.

Persistence is key. In fact, the apostle Paul encouraged the church at Thessalonica to "pray without ceasing" (1 Thessalonians 5:17). That's intense.

To illustrate the importance of persistence in prayer, Jesus told the parable of a widow who kept coming to the judge begging for justice against her adversary. Finally, he gave in to her because she never stopped asking. Jesus then said, "And will not God bring about justice for his chosen ones, who cry out to him day and night? Will he keep putting them off?" (Luke 18:7 NIV).

God loves persistence, and He rewards those who persist.

Just look at the confidence David was given as he sought the Lord even though he was surrounded by lions many times in his life:

> One thing I have asked from the LORD, that I shall seek:
> That I may dwell in the house of the LORD all the days of
>   my life,
> To behold the beauty of the LORD
> And to meditate in His temple.
> For in the day of trouble He will conceal me in His
>   tabernacle;
> In the secret place of His tent He will hide me;
> He will lift me up on a rock.
> And now my head will be lifted up above my enemies
>   around me,
> And I will offer in His tent sacrifices with shouts of joy;
> I will sing, yes, I will sing praises to the LORD.
> —PSALM 27:4–6

Persistent prayer moves God to answer and develops the confidence we need to stand boldly, thriving in the presence of our enemies.

SOVEREIGN GOD AND
SUPERNATURAL PEOPLE

In his book *Power Through Prayer*, E. M. Bounds wrote:

> What the Church needs today is not more machinery or better,
> not new organizations or more and novel methods, but men
> whom the Holy Spirit can use—men of prayer, men mighty in
> prayer. The Holy Spirit does not flow through methods, but
> through men. He does not come on machinery, but on men.
> He does not anoint plans, but men—men of prayer.[4]

Daniel was anointed this way, and we can be too—through
prayer.

No amount of tongue-lashing or debating is going to win the
hearts and souls of people—only a sovereign God at work
through a supernatural people can transform the world. So when
we pray, we must remember to be intimate with the *person* of
God, identify with His *people*, establish the right *posture*, remain
patient, and always stay *persistent*. This is the kind of prayer that
transforms our lives *and* our world.

Even as we wrote this chapter, we both felt God's conviction
to pray more, to continue our conversation with God throughout
the day so we can walk in His strength. We're entering new territory as a nation, and we need an army of warriors who are willing
to fight the battle on their knees first. Let's do this!

CHAPTER 10

THE STRENGTH OF HUMILITY

God is opposed to the proud, but gives grace to the humble.

—JAMES 4:6

 God knows exactly what it takes to bring a person to his knees. We either humble ourselves before God, or He may humble us before men.

I F WE WANT TO pray thriving prayers as Daniel did, ones that call heaven down to earth, then we must humble ourselves when we pray. Daniel 10:12 shows us a key that unlocks the power of prayer: "Since the first day that you set your mind to gain understanding and to *humble yourself* before your God, your words were heard, and I have come in response to them" (NIV).

If we don't humble ourselves, then God will humble us—because He loves us. He wants to pour His grace out, but He won't unless we're humble. If we're going to live as transformers in today's Babylon, we must be soaked in the spirit of humility. So if we don't choose to humble ourselves, God will do it for us. And that usually stings a little!

If you're a young athlete with God-given talent, pride comes easily. When you take your eyes off God and lock them on yourself, pride blinds you from being His man or woman on a mission for His glory. Life becomes all about you. I (David) remember one of the first times God drove this truth home to my heart. Yes, I said "times"—plural. I struggled with this quite often as a kid. (And Jason was no angel either!) I'll step up to confess what a prideful idiot I became and how God had to humble me as a high school athlete.

Jason and I were featured in *Sports Illustrated* as eighth-grade football and basketball players. By God's grace, we had achieved significant success as junior high athletes. So at the next level, "the Benham brothers" were supposed to bring a state championship to our high school. Even though that never happened, I still thought pretty highly of myself at the time.

We worked hard over the summer before our freshman year. So when football season began, we were ready to take on the big boys. We felt strong and fast, and I let others know—especially opposing teams.

One Friday night we faced a tough school that evenly matched us. The stands were packed, and the score was tight. Although I usually played quarterback, I was slotted as a receiver for this game—partly because I had gotten faster over the summer and partly because I couldn't hit the broad side of a barn some nights (though I would never have admitted that).

We huddled up, and our quarterback—my good friend Phil Connatser—called the play. The ball was coming to me. *Showtime!*

The route was a hitch and go. I had to sprint ten steps toward the defensive back, hesitate like I was going to turn and catch a short pass, and then bolt up the sidelines for a deep pass. The play worked beautifully. Phil threw a perfect ball right into my breadbasket. I caught it and took off as the crowd erupted (I can still hear them now). No one could catch me as I blazed toward the end zone, planning my touchdown dance. Suddenly, from behind, two hands grabbed my jersey and slung me to the ground like a rag doll.

What?! Who?! How did that?! How did he . . . ? Those were the jumbled thoughts running through my head. Stunned and still twenty yards from the end zone, I just lay there, trying to catch my breath. I got up and jogged back to our bench, humiliated. I had just gotten "walked down" by some dude that, in my mind, shouldn't have even been on the field that night. (*Jason: I was watching him run down the sideline, and it looked like he hit a five-hundred-mile-per-hour headwind!*)

The high view I had of myself was crushed. God brought me low under the Friday night lights on a football field in Texas with the entire school watching. For me at the time, this one play was a decisive, devastating blow.

I remember Dad used to say to me, "God knows what it takes to bring a proud man low." Well, He knew exactly what would humble me—but only because He loved me. My view of myself was filled with pride, which paralyzed me from having an impact for God's kingdom. I was so focused on myself that I failed to see the value of others, including my opponents.

When I read verses like this, I'm reminded of that night: "He is able to humble those who walk in pride" (Daniel 4:37).

THE PRESENCE PREFERENCE

Webster's 1828 dictionary defines *humility* as "a modest estimate of one's own worth. In theology, *humility* consists of lowliness of mind; a deep sense of one's own unworthiness in the sight of God, self-abasement, penitence for sin, and submission to the divine will."[1]

Daniel's transformed lifestyle was based on this type of humility. (*Jason: A virtue David didn't possess in his football glory days.*) This defining characteristic put him on the path of no resistance toward God and characterized the entire narrative of his life.

Obviously Daniel didn't seem to view himself as highly as we do. Although God gave him powerful talents and influence in Babylon's highest court, Daniel never positioned himself for promotion or tried to "brand" his name. Rather, Daniel saw himself as God's man serving God's purposesw on God's earth. So he left his personal success completely in God's hands.

Daniel had no agenda except to be a lowly servant of the highest King. This position of humility enabled him to walk in supernatural power. He did not pursue gifts, praise, or promotion. So he did not shrink before rivals, laws, or lions.

Daniel did not have to try to be humble. He spent time in God's presence—and nothing creates humility in the human heart like God's presence. As Job testified after encountering God personally,

"I have heard of You by the hearing of the ear;
But now my eye sees You;

> Therefore I retract,
> And I repent in dust and ashes."
>
> —JOB 42:5–6

 Whether in promotion or persecution, God's presence empowers the humbled heart.

The secret to Daniel's humility was his heart and lifestyle of worship, which sought one goal—the presence of almighty God. God's presence and human pride cannot coexist. Daniel walked in God's presence—both when he received promotion and when he experienced persecution—which filled him with power to walk faithfully as a humble champion of God in Babylon.

Daniel knew his life wasn't his own, and he was put on the earth to serve God's purposes. Apart from the presence of God, he could accomplish nothing (Daniel 9:18). And that presence meant more to Daniel than promotion from the king.

HIT PAUSE FOR PRAISE

Daniel's gratitude revealed his humility. His thankfulness was the main barometer of his spirit.

Put yourself in Daniel's shoes for a minute. Can you imagine the president of the United States having a nightmare he desperately wanted interpreted and then God gives you not only the interpretation of the dream but also the details of the dream itself? How would you respond if God showed you this?

Look at what Daniel said the minute he received God's response:

> Daniel answered and said: "Blessed be the name of God for-
> ever and ever, to whom belong wisdom and might. . . . To you,
> O God of my fathers, I give *thanks and praise*, for you have
> given me wisdom and might, and have now made known to
> me what we asked of you."
>
> —DANIEL 2:19–23 ESV

Daniel's humility provoked him to pause and give thanks even though the clock was ticking on his life. He stopped and went to God before he went to the king—simply to thank and praise Him. This is how important thanksgiving was to Daniel. This is a picture of deep, genuine humility.

Humble people give God thanks and praise when they come into His presence. The psalmist said,

> Enter His gates with thanksgiving
> And His courts with praise.
> Give thanks to Him, bless His name.
>
> —PSALM 100:4

I (Jason) was able to teach my oldest son this lesson after one of his basketball games. After watching him play really well in a hoops tournament, I could tell by the way he was acting on the court that pride was starting to set in. But instead of hitting his ego directly, I chose to focus on his gratitude first.

As we drove home, I reminded him of our trip to the Philippines. We had met several families who lived on a dumpsite in huts made of tires and tin. Every day the kids would search for things to eat or sell for money to buy food. That was their life.

They weren't concerned with scoring three-point buckets; they were concerned with landing three dollars' worth of food.

"That could've been you," I told him. "But God chose to put you here with us. And He created you with a talent to bring Him glory—that's why God placed you where He did and gave you talent. Are you thankful to Him for that?"

He looked through the car window as I spoke to him, recalling the vivid scene of those families' living conditions. His little heart broke when we were there. But he had forgotten all about that and put his eyes on himself. Now, as he considered all God had done for him, his heart started to fill with gratitude. And guess what disappeared completely —pride! His attitude totally changed during that car ride.

 When gratitude replaces selfishness, humility replaces pride.

Daniel chose to praise God even before rushing to the king to rescue his own neck (you'll remember that the king had put a death warrant out for "wise men" like Daniel [Daniel 2:13]). But his humility did not end there. It extended all the way to the royal court and his first interaction with the king.

Back to our analogy of the president's dream—let's say you received the interpretation from God and knew you would save many American leaders and be promoted. The president would then ask you, "So, can you tell me the dream and what it means?" What would you have said?

If you're anything like us, you probably would've responded, "Mr. President, your cabinet, councils, and scholars could *never* declare your dream and its interpretation. However, it is my honor as God's man of faith and power to present my interpretation of the dream!" (Wait for applause.)

But not Daniel. His deep-seated humility would not allow him to answer in such a way. He said,

> "As for the mystery about which the king has inquired, neither wise men, conjurers, magicians nor diviners are able to declare it to the king. However, there is a God in heaven who reveals mysteries, and He has made known to King Nebuchadnezzar what will take place in the latter days."
>
> —DANIEL 2: 27–28

"There is a God in heaven." What a humble and profound answer. Daniel totally removed himself so only God got credit for the revelation. That is the way Daniel thought. He viewed this pivotal moment as the perfect opportunity to glorify His God—not himself. Now that's humility on steroids!

Daniel removed himself from the equation so the transaction could be between God and the king. He decreased his personal position to proclaim the king's mystery with power—and God received all the glory. It perfectly brings to life the declaration from John the Baptist: "He must increase, but I must decrease" (John 3:30).

Had Daniel approached the king seeking his own glory, the king might have responded with praise for Daniel. But because of his humility, the king responded with praise to God: "Surely your God is a God of gods and a Lord of kings and a revealer of mysteries, since you have been able to reveal this mystery" (Daniel 2:47).

Daniel sought the glory of God and the good of others over himself because humility's main goal, ultimately, is to glorify God.

PRAY, SEEK, TURN

As we discussed in chapter 9, Daniel's prayer for his people in Daniel 9 is one of the most humble prayers in the Bible because Daniel assumed responsibility for not only his own sins but also those of all God's people, saying, "we have sinned, we have been wicked. O Lord, in accordance with all Your righteous acts, let now Your anger and Your wrath turn away from Your city Jerusalem" (vv. 15–16). He bowed in self-abasement with those who had gone before him. He begged forgiveness for *our* sins—including, as we said before, those committed before he was even born.

 Humility is the first step toward healing. And healing—both personally and in community—is a transformational process. Humility opens the door for transformation to begin.

Daniel knew the Scriptures well, so he understood what God required if His people sinned and fell under judgment. Look again at 2 Chronicles 7:14, and see what Daniel likely saw:

And my people who are called by My name *humble* themselves and pray and seek My face and turn from their wicked ways, then I will hear from heaven, will forgive their sin and will heal their land.

Knowing this truth, Daniel continually bowed in humility as part of his identity.

Those first few words in 2 Chronicles 7:14 show us something about God's people and humility—it's one of the most powerful combinations on earth. Put them together, and you have all the power in heaven to move mountains, shake nations, destroy strongholds, and transform the world.

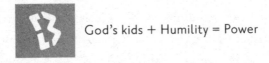 God's kids + Humility = Power

How was Daniel able to withstand human pride when he was promoted to third in the kingdom? Humility.

How was he able to keep from wallowing in pity when he was persecuted for his faith? Humility.

What quality came forth from Daniel's heart, allowing God to answer his prayer on behalf of his nation? Humility.

How was he able to live faithfully and powerfully, transforming Babylon for God's glory? Pride. Just kidding—making sure we keep you on your toes. It was humility!

THE BIG I IN PRIDE

We repeat: God's presence and human pride cannot coexist. Pride is the opposite of humility, and it is a killer that God hates. In Proverbs 8:13, the Lord said, "I hate pride and arrogance" (NIV). Um, call us crazy, but if God—the Author of Love—hates something, we might want to check ourselves before we wreck ourselves.

God resists the proud, but gives grace to the humble (James 4:6). Nothing could be worse than the God of heaven resisting you. Look at our culture today. Can you see God resisting us? Despite billions of dollars spent in government programs, we continue our slide downward economically, socially, and morally. Jeremiah's words ring true today:

> "My people have committed two evils:
> They have forsaken Me,
> The fountain of living waters,
> To hew for themselves cisterns,
> Broken cisterns
> That can hold no water."
>
> —JEREMIAH 2:13

No matter how many humanitarian programs and government dollars we throw at our problems, our pride has created a separation between our nation and God's presence (Isaiah 59:2).

Pride demands rights while minimizing responsibility—classic self-centered living versus God-centered living. Pride walks over people to climb the ladder of success and is not willing to serve or put others first.

How does pride grow? By comparing ourselves to the wrong people. *Jesus* is our standard, not other people. Humility means following Jesus, using His life as our barometer, and refusing to compare ourselves to others.

Sheep look white . . . until it snows. Then you realize how dirty they truly are. We may look and feel as though we're good when compared to others—until we compare ourselves to God. Then we become humbled pretty quickly.

When Isaiah saw God, the first words out of his mouth were "Woe is me, for I am ruined! Because I am a man of unclean lips" (Isaiah 6:5). And this guy was a prophet of God! If he was saying this when he entered God's presence, how much more will we?

Humility causes us to compare ourselves to God and allows the stinging conviction that shapes us into Christlike people. Pride is comparing ourselves to others so we can be exalted without paying the price.

Chip Ingram wrote, "Comparing ourselves with others and deciding that we are in some way inferior—that we come up short or got the raw end of the deal when God handed out gifts and blessings—may look like humility at times but actually leads to bitterness and resentment. And comparing ourselves and deciding that we are in some way superior—that we are more highly favored or more inherently valuable—is arrogance."[2] Can you see how dangerous this is to compare yourself to others? It's a recipe for sin.

So the next time you are tempted toward pride or envy by comparing yourself to someone, stop. Then take your eyes off the person and put them on God. This split-second decision will bring humility to your heart. Considering God makes all the difference.

> When I consider Your heavens, the work of Your fingers,
> The moon and the stars, which You have ordained;
> What is man that You take thought of him,
> And the son of man that You care for him?
>
> —PSALM 8:3–4

DEMOTION TO DEVOTION

My (Jason's) first job after I retired from professional baseball was as a ministry consultant for John Maxwell's leadership training company. "Ministry consultant" was basically a nice way of saying "inside sales." All day long I sat in a cubicle with a headset on, staring at a computer screen. How do you say "culture shock"?

This was actually a great job, and I was surrounded by some amazing people, but I was really struggling for two reasons. First, my identity was still wrapped up in being a professional athlete, so having a "normal job" was a shot to my ego. Second, I was the worst salesperson on the team, but I was used to being one of the best on *any* team.

One day I got a phone call from David while he was at spring training. He called to tell me his manager told him if he stayed healthy, he was a shoo-in for the big leagues. Here I was sitting in my cubicle, rocking business casual, listening to my twin brother tell me about his success in pro ball, and all the while I could hear the crack of the bat in the background. Every hit was going straight to my heart.

God was taking me to my knees. I prided myself in making a living as an athlete—that was where my identity was. But that pride was now gone, and my brother had just stomped on it. (Thanks, dude.)

While David was on the fast track to the majors, I was on the slow track to success as a salesperson. I was on a team with six other people, two of whom were grandmothers, and one twenty-one-year-old hyperactive guy. Every day we would record our sales to track our productivity as a team and as individuals.

I was always dead last. Although I was trying my best, I couldn't sell squat!

I quickly became "that guy"—you know, the one who never plays until the end of a mop-up game? It was humiliating. The two grandmas were always so nice to me. They would see my numbers compared to theirs, put their arms around me, and say, "It's okay, Jason. You'll catch on. We believe in you."

God knew I needed those two ladies in my life at that moment because just as soon as they took their arms off me, the twenty-one-year-old kid would walk up with a little grin on his face. I could tell he was basking in the thrill of dominating me . . . every single day. But God knew I needed him in my life too. I just didn't realize it yet. God had gifted this guy with his mouth. He could sell ice to an Eskimo. If you ever got into a debate with him, he would walk you down and finish you off right in front of everyone. So here I was, getting dominated by a guy way younger than me whom I couldn't even argue with!

What in the world was God doing with me? Why was He allowing this to happen? I felt like such a loser. For me at the time, I was at rock bottom.

Then one day the truth hit me as I was praying before work. God wanted me here in *this* position doing *this* job around *these* people. Everything about where I was and what I was doing was His doing. I was a player on His team now. God didn't want me taking pride in what I did for a living or getting caught up comparing myself to those around me. He just wanted me to be a faithful servant, which was impossible apart from humility. I got on my knees and asked God to forgive my pride and help me see this job from His perspective.

For the next few months I was a different person. While I

still wasn't thrilled about the job itself, I began to see the beauty of where I was. I was actually thankful I had a job and began to appreciate all those people God put on my team. Yes, even the hyper whiz kid! We actually became good friends, and he taught me a lot of his tricks. (I can't share those with you, or I'd have to kill you.)

Two months later a friend in Charlotte offered me a job as a ministry coordinator for a large Christian company. God had done His work *on* me, and now it was time for Him to work *through* me. He knew I needed this short period in my life to strip me down and get me closer to the end of myself. This was the firmest foundation I could ever stand on. My path from consultant to coordinator had to go through the tunnel of humility.

PRUNING OUT PRIDE

Humility is so crucial to a transformed lifestyle that God will take us through seasons of tremendous pruning, stripping, and loss to humble us. (*David: I became a janitor after playing pro baseball!*) We are too valuable to Him to be filled with pride. He will risk our disappointment to take us down a hard road because humility is far more important than success.

So if you're going through such a period now, allow God to have His way. Value humility above all, and allow God to exalt you in His time (1 Peter 5:6). Daniel went through periods like this (being exiled and threatened with death), yet God exalted him—all because He desires to pour Himself into us so the world might know that He is God.

God wants to pour His grace out on us, both personally and

as a nation—a grace that is so amazing it cannot be explained. But He doesn't stop there—He will also pour this gift upon any one or any nation that honors and exalts Him as King.

Do we want to receive God's favor and blessing? The first step is through the door of humility. And when we humble ourselves and live there, as Daniel did, not only does God hear our prayers, but He also responds. "Then he said to me, 'Do not be afraid, Daniel, for from the first day that you set your heart on understanding this and on *humbling* yourself before your God, your words were heard, and I have come in response to your words'" (Daniel 10:12).

Every follower of Jesus is going to go through the pruning process multiple times in life. God uses this to trim the world out of us and put more of Him in us. This loving discipline from God takes us to a stronger level of humility, squeezing out more pride. While being humbled is never any fun, the end result is worth the pain because this purifies our hearts and minds. It makes us more useful to God and more available to our neighbors in Babylon.

CHAPTER 11

THE POWER OF PURITY

Who gave Himself for us to redeem us from every lawless deed, and to purify for Himself a people for His own possession, zealous for good deeds.

—TITUS 2:14

 God calls us to be lightning bolts, not lightning bugs.

WHEN WE WERE EIGHT, there was a huge storm late one summer night in Dallas, and lightning struck dozens of trees around our neighborhood. We'll never forget when a bolt hit our big maple in the front yard, snapping the tree nearly in half. The *crack* was crazy loud! (*David: Jason actually started bawling and tried to crawl into bed with me, but I would have none of that.*)

After the storm was over, we went into the front yard to look. The tree was charred like it had been on a barbecue grill. Massive branches lay on the ground. The sight was surreal. But the most striking part (pun intended) was how crisp and clean the air had become. For summers in Texas, this was not the norm. The atmosphere was no longer hot and humid, but cool and fresh.

Aside from Jason's near meltdown, our first big experience with lightning was pretty cool. This experience also eventually taught us a vital kingdom principle. God uses lightning to purify the air. These natural, electric bolts do more than generate power. Research shows they produce significant amounts of oxidants that help to clean up the atmosphere.[1]

God has given us His Spirit so we can have the same effect. He has called us to be lightning bolts—powerful points of light that purify the environment. But too often we act like little lightning bugs, just floating by and blinking with no real impact.

So how do we go from lightning bugs to lightning bolts? By getting rid of the things that don't belong in our lives. This produces powerful purity. Remember how, early in Daniel's life, he and his friends refused to be defiled with the king's food (Daniel 1:8)? They knew that what the king was offering them represented more than simply physical nourishment; it was a total program of assimilation into Babylon's culture, spiritually and morally. So they started refusing just one impure thing, and their resolve was a powerful commitment to personal purity.

 To be powerful purifiers, we must first be personally pure.

Daniel and his friends' lifestyle empowered them to transform the air in Babylon. Their purity pleased God and led to God's blessing. God's blessing led to supernatural wisdom and insight into the king's dreams. And that insight invaded the king's court like flashes of lightning. See the path of the striking bolt? From heaven to earth!

Later in Daniel's life he struck like lightning into King

Belshazzar's drunken party, purifying the air with the crisp clarity of God's message to the king (Daniel 5). Daniel was an older man when this other king of Babylon took the sacred Jewish cups meant for religious purposes and used them to get drunk at his pagan party. Suddenly God's hand appeared in the room, writing Belshazzar's judgment on the wall.

When Daniel was summoned to interpret the writing, the king offered him gifts for his interpretation, but he held on to his inner resolve to be personally pure: "Keep your gifts for yourself or give your rewards to someone else," he said (v. 17). He kept himself free from self-promotion, which allowed him to strike with precision and power, generating a considerable change in the air. The party went from reveling to reverence when Daniel arrived.

Daniel transformed the atmosphere of Babylon because he had transformed the atmosphere of his own lifestyle first. He was a powerful purifier amid Babylon's spiritually polluted environment.

PURITY AND POISON

Satan hates Christians because we threaten to purify the spiritual atmosphere he works so hard to pollute. He tries to corrupt the atmosphere *inside* of us so we can't purify the atmosphere *outside* of us. He tempts us in two ways: with the passing pleasures of sin and with the attractions of powerless religion in place of genuine faith. Either or both of these satanic ingredients compromise our own purity as well as our ability to purify our atmosphere.

Therefore, one of the Enemy's greatest weapons against our

purity is *mixture*. We'll explain. Satan often sneaks tiny compromises into our hearts rather than trying to drag us into blatant sin. Why the subtlety? These compromises are harder to detect, and we can feel as though we're not really sinning "that bad." But that little mixture in our hearts dilutes our purifying power, continuing to slowly and quietly grow and spread beneath our conviction. All the while it makes us feel as though we're not doing anything really bad. If undetected and not handed over to the Lord, in the end, this tactic works, causing us to act like lightning bugs, not lightning bolts.

Small compromises are like undiagnosed viruses; they can spread through you undetected until deadly. The Bible uses a baking metaphor for this principle: "A little leaven leavens the whole lump of dough" (Galatians 5:9). A modern version of that little parable might be this: "One drop of poison in a gallon of water poisons the whole container, no matter how pure the water was before." Would you want to drink from a gallon of water that *was* perfectly pure, but you knew it now contained just one drop of fatal poison?

Though we believers must mix in with culture *externally* (like a chocolate chip in cookie dough), we must not allow the culture to mix in with us *internally*. Transformational purity requires us to guard our hearts and lifestyles from the world's infiltration.

As tiny cracks in a dam eventually give way to the pressure of the water, mixture in our lives can render us powerless to stand against the pressures of the culture. But purity maintains God's rule for God's kingdom in our hearts and enables us to stand firm. This is why the apostle Paul was so militant in his approach toward mixture in our minds: "We are destroying speculations and every lofty thing raised up against the knowledge of God, and we are taking every thought captive to the obedience of Christ" (2 Corinthians 10:5).

We *take captive* every thought, not allowing it to make itself at home in our minds and pollute the purity and clarity of God's truth. The moment we allow just a bit of mixture, the pressure to conform will soon overtake us.

 Mixing a love for God with a love for the world is the quickest way to turn a hero into a zero, a warrior into a wimp.

Though he was living among Babylon's moral and spiritual pollution, Daniel refused to allow its ways to mix into his heart and mind. He would not take in the accursed things of Babylon. As a result, he was a lightning bolt, constantly striking a pagan land with heaven's purity.

LIFE ON THE ALTAR

So how can we live with lightning impact in today's Babylon? We must be holy as God is holy (1 Peter 1:16) and have "clean hands and a pure heart" (Psalm 24:4). We must commit ourselves to purity, not with occasional events but as a lifestyle.

Jesus defined purity not only by physical acts but also by thoughts. In His teaching, Jesus essentially redefined adultery to be not just a physical act but one committed in the mind: "But I say to you that everyone who looks at a woman with lust for her has already committed adultery with her in his heart" (Matthew 5:28).

Biblical purity, then, is actually for our *entire* being, not just our bodies. Where does murder begin? Where does theft begin? Where does lying begin? All start with an emotion, a motive, an attitude that eventually, if left unchecked, becomes an action. Paul warned us to "take every thought captive" (2 Corinthians 10:5 ESV)—to kill the seed before the sprouting of the weed.

So how do we keep our hearts pure? Two areas of daily focus empower us to a lifestyle of both inner and outer purity.

1. Commit to offer yourself as a living sacrifice.

Therefore I urge you, brethren, by the mercies of God, to present your bodies a living and holy sacrifice, acceptable to God, which is your spiritual service of worship. (Romans 12:1)

This verse is quoted often and is very familiar in Christian circles, so we can easily miss its strong message. The very nature of a sacrifice means it must die. A sacrifice was killed and then placed on the altar. But Paul placed the word *living* in front of *sacrifice*, making it an oxymoron. How can something designated to die still live? Only by staying on the altar of sacrifice, choosing to die to sin and to ourselves at *all* times, can we surrender as a living sacrifice.

 The temptation is to crawl off the altar when the heat turns up. But if we stay on the altar, constantly sacrificing our own thoughts, attitudes, actions, and motives, purity becomes not a work we do but a way we live.

2. Commit to walk in the power of the Holy Spirit.

Paul challenged the Corinthian church in their purity by saying: "Or do you not know that your body is a temple of the Holy Spirit who is in you, whom you have from God, and that you are not your own? For you have been bought with a price: therefore glorify God in your body" (1 Corinthians 6:19–20).

God's own presence abides within every Christian. He gave us power to live purely in our hearts and behavior. We are literally housing Jesus, walking temples.

But we still have the ability to choose sin over Him. We can grieve the Holy Spirit just like a child grieves a parent, by refusing to listen to the voice of our conscience. So each day we must deliberately submit our minds to the power of the Holy Spirit who lives within us. The power to live in purity is not found in trying harder or in being perfect but in surrendering our will to God for Him to work through us.

Is being pure a tough choice to make in today's culture? Yes. But God calls us to be living sacrifices (step 1) and empowers us to walk as "temples of the Holy Spirit" (step 2).

Living in purity like this will yield three specific things:

I. Power
> He who loves purity of heart
>> And whose speech is gracious, the king
>>> is his friend. (Proverbs 22:11)

When we say "power," we aren't talking about the power to do whatever we *want*, but power to do what we *ought*—what is right and best as God leads. True power brings correction, not corruption, to the environment. This was proven time and again as Daniel attracted the king's ear for counsel.

Purity leads to influence the way lightning strikes with air-cleansing power.

2. Clarity

Blessed are the pure in heart, for they shall see God. (Matthew 5:8)

Those who walk in purity have the ability to discern God's will. When culture presents a mixture of good and evil to trick them out of their convictions, they can distinguish between truth and lies. Pure hearts do not have divided loyalties. Life consists of "the simplicity and purity of devotion to Christ" (2 Corinthians 11:3). Eliminating all allegiances to Babylon maintains a clear line of sight to God and His purposes in the world.

3. Value

Righteous lips are the delight of kings,
And he who speaks right is loved. (Proverbs 16:13)

Gold, silver, diamonds, any precious metals or gems—the greater their purity, the greater their value. Daniel's pure motives, words, and actions brought great value both to the earthly king and the heavenly King—"on earth as it is in heaven" (Matthew 6:10). His purity made him a valuable man of "high esteem." God's angel said to him, "O Daniel, man of high esteem, understand the words that I am about to tell you and stand upright, for I have now been sent to you" (Daniel 10:11). He was pure, so he was deemed worthy to receive God's message.

We are to be living sacrifices and walking temples so we can experience the power, clarity, and value of purity. Purity frees us to be men and women who courageously live lives of transformation in a culture that promotes mixture at every turn.

THE FIRES OF FAITH

Lightning sparks fires. God uses personal lightning storms to purify us from the poisoning influence of the world. Then He uses us to purify the atmosphere, so we must embrace the storms that purify us.

 If you desire a life of purity, then you must embrace the storms that purify.

Before the lightning touched Babylon, God's own bolts had to strike His people in Babylon. The fiery furnace was concocted as an *opposition* to Daniel's friends but became an *opportunity* for God to test their worth and mold them into His image. Fire, after all, is a purifier. The apostle Peter explained, "Beloved, do not be surprised at the fiery ordeal among you, which comes upon you for your testing, as though some strange thing were happening to you" (1 Peter 4:12).

Peter went on to explain the two types of "fiery ordeals":

1. The one we bring upon ourselves because of impurity—sin.

Make sure that none of you suffers as a murderer, or thief, or evildoer, or a troublesome meddler. (v. 15)

2. The one that comes upon us because of purity—faithfulness.

But if anyone suffers as a Christian, he is not to be ashamed, but is to glorify God in this name. (v. 16)

Each one of us has a choice as to which type of storm we will experience. We can suffer for our sin or for our faithfulness. In either situation, God uses the storm to purify us. But the choice is ours.

These storms are not always for individuals. God will also allow larger storms to purify His people as a whole. He wants His bride—the church—to be powerful and pure and without blemish (Ephesians 5:27). Peter directed comments about fiery ordeals to the group: "For it is time for judgment to begin with the *household of God*" (1 Peter 4:17).

Daniel understood the storm of Babylonian captivity was God's judgment on His people for rejecting Him. But Daniel also knew the storm would help *purify* them as a people so God could once again have mercy and give them hope and a future as a nation. Even in their exile, they could hold on to God's promise in Jeremiah: "'For I know the plans that I have for you,' declares the LORD, 'plans for welfare and not for calamity to give you a future and a hope'" (29:11).

To live among lions today, we must first embrace the storm that purifies—pursuing purity on the inside so we can live purely on the outside.

Remember Dr. Lutzer's question that we wrote about earlier: "What does faithfulness look like in the midst of God's judgment?" For the people of Judah, this meant embracing the storm, allowing purification of their hearts, and then living in the power of that purity while in Babylon. In fact, one of the reasons the book of Daniel was written was to show God's people what this process actually looks like. Daniel proved his faithfulness by embracing the storm that purifies inwardly and then living with purity outwardly. He transformed the atmosphere around him for God's glory.

FACING THE FLAMES

Daniel stands as a man of humility, excellence, and purity. Yet the fires still came.

We watch Daniel pass through a number of fiery trials—tests to prove his faithfulness. And his friends went through a literal fiery trial. But all of them were able to endure because they first withstood the flames of temptation in their own hearts.

When we have been purified by God's flame on the inside, we will be untouched by man's furnace on the outside.

When Daniel had to face the lions, he knew he had done nothing wrong. His innocence before God gave him courage to stand his ground in the face of evil. This gave him clarity to discern God's righteous path for him under the shadow of the king's new law.

The moment we allow Babylon to mix in and dilute our purity, our boldness runs for the sidelines. When cowardice replaces courage, we become like the "one thousand" men Isaiah said would "flee at the threat of one man" (Isaiah 30:17). Or we flee even "when no one is pursuing" (Proverbs 28:1).

Can you see this kind of cowardice today? A lack of courage is all too common among God's people in America. Like a pastor who refuses to address cultural hot topics for fear of ridicule, some Christians today are running from the threat of even so much as a frown.

But if we maintain our purity, both personally and corporately, courage will replace cowardice. We'll stand when others are running. We'll become like those Joshua spoke of who cling to the Lord their God—"One of your men puts to flight a thousand, for the LORD your God is He who fights for you" (Joshua 23:10). And we just might change the atmosphere!

So which one will we choose?

SUGAR OR SALT?

God's people must commit not only to personal purity but also purity of the gospel.

We've talked about how the Devil contaminates our effectiveness in the culture with just a "little leaven," a tiny virus, a drop of poison. But sometimes it can be difficult to tell what poison is and what it is not. Contamination involves something real that gets messed up. But a *counterfeit* is fundamentally fake from the beginning.

The apostle Paul warned the Corinthian church about counterfeits when he said, "If one comes and preaches *another* Jesus whom we have not preached, or you receive a different spirit which you have not received, or a different gospel which you have not accepted, you bear this beautifully" (2 Corinthians 11:4). Paul was not complimenting them by saying, "you bear this beautifully," but rather he was warning them against fake apostles desiring to lead them astray.

The most dangerous counterfeit is the one that looks identical to the real thing. It's like trying to tell the difference between sugar and salt. To the eye, they're identical—until put to the test. Rub sugar on a steak and do the same with salt. Come back in a few days and look at the difference. The salt preserves while the sugar corrupts.

Counterfeit Christians are like sugar. They are men and women who look identical to the real thing yet preach a different gospel. They talk about Jesus, yet mix the Bible with the world's teachings. The pure gospel is distorted, which renders it useless in working as salt in Christians' lives and in fighting against the gates of hell.

Here are two ways you can identify a counterfeit:

1. Counterfeits deny the inerrancy of the Bible.
2. Counterfeits refuse to accept the sovereignty of God.

As a result of this doctrinal disrespect, they distort the truth in two important ways:

1. How they deal with sin. They deny its impact, stay silent regarding its reality, and redefine biblical teachings to suit their lifestyle (or the cultural norm).
2. How they deal with self. They put self at the center and God as our "helper" to a happy life.

We're pretty certain Daniel would not be a fan of today's contaminated or counterfeit gospel.

When the church remains committed to the inerrancy of God's Word and surrendered to God's sovereignty and establishes a biblical view on sin and self, it has all the power to strike the culture as a powerful purifier.

CLARITY AND COURAGE

Daniel brought clarity and courage to a culture where confusion and fear ruled the day. He was the same man on the inside that he was on the outside. This gave him all the strength he needed to stand with courage and not give way to the wicked.

So when Satan shows up in your life with a little mixture of the world, don't give in! Like Daniel, you must resolve in your heart not to be defiled, no matter the cost. Truth blended with a little lie is not truth but mixture. Jesus—plus or minus anything—is not Jesus but mixture.

Let's bring back a truth from chapter 8: our only offensive

weapon to resist Satan's allures toward mixture is the Word of God. The psalmist wrote:

> How can a young man keep his way pure?
> By keeping it according to Your word.
>
> —PSALM 119:9

Just as Jesus countered the lies of the Devil with the truth of God's Word when tempted (Matthew 4:1–11), we can do the same by wielding the power of the sword. As we reply "It is written" when tempted, we have the same power to overcome that Christ had.

No more mixture but only purity. Let's wield the Spirit's sword and sever the lies. Remember Daniel risked his neck to remain committed to purity. But this resulted in his eternal impact on Babylon's kingdom. We, too, can be lightning bolts that strike our Babylon, cleansing and refreshing its atmosphere. But we must commit to purity as a lifestyle, as the church, and in our gospel—whatever the cost.

PART III

COURAGE THAT TRANSFORMS MY WORLD

W E CAN'T HELP BUT start this section with some courageous
words of wisdom:

> If I profess, with the loudest voice and clearest exposition,
> every portion of the truth of God except precisely that little
> point which the world and the devil are at that moment
> attacking, I am not confessing Christ, however boldly I may
> be professing Christianity. Where the battle rages the loyalty
> of the soldier is proved; and to be steady on all the battle-field
> besides, is mere flight and disgrace to him if he flinches at
> that one point.
>
> —ELIZABETH RUNDLE CHARLES[1]

We've pointed out the important things that allowed Daniel
to have courage to transform his world. Now we'll take a closer
look at what that courage looked like and how we can build it in

our own lives. This is the part of Daniel's story that makes us want to jump out of our chairs, slap on the blue face paint from *Braveheart*, and shout "Freedom!" at the top of our lungs!

Our favorite line from that movie was "Every man dies. But not every man truly lives."[2] In the same vein, Martin Luther King Jr. said, "A man dies when he refuses to stand up for that which is right."[3]

By living with the same conviction and commitment of Daniel, we, too, can stand up for that which is right. But this takes courage. Daniel and his friends show us that as crucial as conviction and commitment are, these two kingdom life principles are incomplete by themselves. Courage is the last element—the final note in our spiritual triad that enables us to *truly live* by transforming our world.

Part three unfolds the crucial elements of Daniel and his friends' courage:

A Hard Head and a Soft Heart
Let It Be Known
Keep the Windows Open
"Keep Your Gifts"
Seek the Welfare of the City
Face the Lions

CHAPTER 12

A HARD HEAD AND
A SOFT HEART

*"Like emery harder than flint I have made your forehead. Do
not be afraid of them or be dismayed before them."*

—Ezekiel 3:9

*"Moreover, I will give you a new heart and put a new
spirit within you; and I will remove the heart of stone
from your flesh and give you a heart of flesh."*

—Ezekiel 36:26

 When we have God's heart toward individuals and
God's mind toward ideas, we have a responsibility
to be God's mouth in culture.

B EFORE WE JUMP INTO the third section of our book about
courage, let's revisit our baseball analogy. When we have a
talent to play the game (conviction) coupled with a solid work

173

ethic to be the best at the sport (commitment), we then have to go out there and play the game (courage). And when we set foot on the field, we swing for the fences!

Daniel stepped onto Babylon's field and did just that.

As we discussed in chapter 7, our playing field is right where God has placed us—with our family, friends, workplace, and community—in our world. When we're faithful to transform our own little world, God then allows us to take part in transforming the rest of the world—our city, our state, our nation, and ultimately the whole earth.

God has equipped us to be His agents of transformation in the world. But how do we do this in a world where evil is called good and good is called evil? How do we interact with those who not only disagree with us but actually oppose us?

Courage!

> Be strong and courageous, do not be afraid or tremble at them, for the LORD your God is the one who goes with you. He will not fail you or forsake you.
>
> —DEUTERONOMY 31:6

We can't just be content with conviction and commitment. We need the courage to step on the field to swing—and swing hard! So after we build our conviction and commitment, how can we foster the same kind of courage Daniel had in Babylon?

We must have a hard head and a soft heart.

Yes, we know this sounds odd, but just sit tight and keep reading—we'll explain.

A soft heart means that the motive behind our courage is not self-righteous frustration, but *love*—genuine love for God and love for people.

A hard head means that our goal is to please God, not man—to stand firmly on His principles and timeless truths, regardless of what others say or do.

Oswald Chambers summed it up nicely: "Never water down the word of God, preach it in its undiluted sternness; there must be unflinching loyalty to the word of God; but when you come to personal dealing with your fellow men, remember who you are—not a special being made up in heaven, but a sinner saved by grace."[1]

 Soft heart + Hard head = Courage

In today's volatile and sometimes hostile culture, if we don't have a soft heart and a hard head, we have little chance to transform anyone's world—including our own.

BEING BIBLICALLY BALANCED

Daniel displayed a soft heart and a hard head when he interpreted Nebuchadnezzar's second dream. He had the courage to tell the king that God was about to judge him. But his heart was so soft toward Nebuchadnezzar as a human being that he delivered the bad news with genuine compassion. This was the same king who destroyed Daniel's nation!

Notice Daniel's grace-filled language here: "My lord, if only the dream applied to those who hate you and its interpretation to your adversaries! . . . Therefore, O king, may my advice be pleasing to you: break away now from your sins . . . in case there may be a prolonging of your prosperity" (Daniel 4:19, 27).

Daniel's head was hard enough to tell the king what he needed to hear, not what he wanted to hear. But his heart was soft enough to approach the king as a friend and to desire his well-being. Daniel's heart burned with compassion toward the man. But his head barreled through any fear of that man.

Softheartedness by itself becomes people-pleasing. Hard-headedness without compassion becomes mean-spirited and angry. Erring to the extreme on either side can be easy, but good leaders embrace the tension between the two and live it out. That is courage.

LOVE LANGUAGE

Religious pressure in America today has occurred largely in the realm of ideas. These ideas are concepts, opinions, and beliefs that people hold to be true or real. Ideas lead to behavior, and behaviors lead to consequences. God cares about ideas—and so should we (Psalm 51:6; 139:2).

Some ideas are contrary to God's Word and against His best for our lives. Yet people hold on to them firmly. They don't realize that those ideas keep them in bondage. So if we're going to be a part of God's plan to transform people through the gospel, then we must address their ideas—even those ideas that define them while holding them captive.

God loves all people, but He does not love all ideas.

If we have a hard heart, we will approach people's ideas with the goal of simply making our point—or getting them to think like us. That's never a good plan. But if we have a soft heart, we'll approach them with compassion, wanting God's best. The only problem with being softhearted is it's easy to keep quiet for fear of offending people. The solution is to develop a *soft* heart and a *hard* head.

> But speaking the truth in love, we are to grow up in all aspects into Him who is the head, even Christ.
>
> —EPHESIANS 4:15

Notice how Paul placed truth (the hard head) and love (the soft heart) together in strong partnership.

After a disappointing experience with our reality-TV show, we had the chance to learn this firsthand. God used this situation to push us out of our safe little comfort zone and put us smack-dab in the middle of a media firestorm. We knew Jesus taught us to love our enemies and pray for those who persecute us. But not until we were actually thrown into the fires did we understand how this works. The amazing thing is, as the interviews and controversy swirled, we really felt love toward those who were criticizing us. We can only attribute this to the Holy Spirit.

Jesus taught us not to worry beforehand about what to say when we are falsely accused and brought before governing authorities. In those moments, the Holy Spirit will give us the words to speak (Mark 13:11). But we didn't know exactly how all that worked until this time in our lives.

We discovered that this genuine love for the people targeting us paved the way for God's Spirit to speak through us. It was surreal—God guided us *through love*. Again, this was the work of the Holy Spirit. Nothing in our flesh could have drummed up an emotion that strong in those tough moments. That is why we never had anything hateful to say toward anyone. We actually felt genuine love and concern for all the people coming against us. God gave us soft hearts toward those slamming us.

But love doesn't stop with a feeling. Love always takes action to serve the other person's best interest.

This is where the hard head comes in. While we felt genuine love toward people, we also experienced a righteous anger toward the ideas that held them captive. And a hard head can't help but speak up. "We are destroying speculations and every lofty thing raised up against the knowledge of God, and we are taking every thought captive to the obedience of Christ" (2 Corinthians 10:5).

Although we went to war in the realm of ideas, God empowered us to remain softhearted toward the people who held those ideas.

A Christian boldly resists the ideas exalted against the knowledge of God but reaches out with compassion to the people who hold them.

Our first interview was on CNN. We had plenty of opportunities to slam those attacking us, but we didn't. After we finished the interview, the anchor came back on the line and told us she was surprised at how gracious we were during the interview. Her response solidified our resolve to keep soft hearts and hard heads. The Lord used that interview to equip us for the long road ahead.

THE GREATEST OF THESE

During our first book tour, we met many Christian leaders who have large platforms to communicate their faith. But they often get disoriented when their biblical worldview faces conflict on the battlefield of ideas. At a conference near the end of our tour, one leader asked us, "If I do a national TV interview with a panel of guests diametrically opposed to my beliefs, how do I keep from offending them while still communicating the truth?"

Several others asked similar difficult questions. They don't want to hurt anyone's feelings. But by choosing diplomacy, many Christians have simply remained quiet. We understand that pressure. But here's how the Lord taught us to approach this.

We responded, "You cannot go into such a situation strictly with your head. And you certainly can't let your head point the way. You have to let your heart lead the interview. Your primary objective is to minister to those who oppose you without compromising the truth.

"Imagine you are at a church altar, praying with these people to receive Jesus. When they present ideas contrary to God's Word, don't try to win the debate. Overcome them with the *heart* of God's Word—the heart of God the Father who *loves* them and longs for them to experience freedom. Your ultimate goal is their restoration in Christ. Without bringing your heart to the table, you cannot accomplish this.

"But you also don't leave your head behind either. Just don't let it lead. You must have a soft heart and a hard head—love the *people* but speak God's truth against any idea that would keep them from coming to the knowledge of Christ."

This applies to *every* area of life, not just the culture wars.

When we started our business, we had no clue what "measurable metrics" were. We didn't know how to gauge our success other than by how many clients we landed and how much money we made. But as we studied Scripture, we felt the Holy Spirit say, *Serve with your heart first, and touch the hearts of the people you serve.* We were already committed to the business truth of excellence in client satisfaction with a hardheaded resolve. But how were we supposed to measure serving with our hearts?

We decided our goal would be to hear clients say they loved us, enjoyed working with us, and felt valued. We wanted them to feel that we truly cared about them and not just keeping their business.

One of our first measurable metric e-mails came from a client in Florida. He was one of our best customers at the time. He said he loved us both and felt as though we were family. *Boom!* Now *that* was an awesome feeling.

There can be a tendency to take this approach too far. A stubborn commitment to hardheaded excellence is the perfect counterweight to leading with your heart in business. But as we applied this paradigm of measuring success by the personal impact we had on people, our business exploded. And many of the relationships we built over the years are still going strong today.

If we're going to be effective witnesses in the world, then we must have soft hearts *and* hard heads. This is true in our families, our businesses, and everyday interaction in our communities.

PROPHET MARGIN

Zechariah and Ezekiel were two prophets who revealed God's desire for a soft heart and a hard head. God sent them with difficult messages at different times in Israel's history. In every generation, representing God's truth in cultures opposed or indifferent to Him has been difficult. This certainly didn't make these prophets the most popular guys in town. Notice the contrast in what God spoke to each of them:

> "They made their *hearts like flint* so that they could not hear the law and the words which the LORD of hosts had sent by His Spirit through the former prophets; therefore great wrath came from the LORD of hosts."
>
> —ZECHARIAH 7:12

> "Like emery *harder than flint* I have made *your forehead.* Do not be afraid of them or be dismayed before them, though they are a rebellious house."
>
> —EZEKIEL 3:9

In the Zechariah passage, the Jews had made their own hearts hard, but in Ezekiel, God made the prophet's head hard. It's easy to see which had the better result. God told Zechariah that the Jews could no longer hear the words that brought life, healing, and hope because they had hardened their hearts. The result was pain and death.

Our hearts become hard when we disobey God and continue in rebellion. Deliberate sin hardens the heart, blocks the ears, and then dims the eyes. We can't hear as God hears or see as God sees.

Then we see God tell Ezekiel He was going to make his head hard because of the backlash he would experience from the people. God didn't want Ezekiel fazed by their words. When the labels started to fly—"bigot," "hater"—he would have courage.

 The softer our hearts grow toward God, the harder our heads should grow toward evil—in our own lives and in the culture around us.

We also see this in Jesus' life: "When the days were approaching for His ascension, He was determined to go to Jerusalem" (Luke 9:51). Even though He was sure to face trouble, He was set on facing the beatings and His own death for us. Many commentators say that Christ "set His face like a flint" to go to His crucifixion. Like the prophets before Him, He hardened His head and determined to move toward the cross—whatever the cost. *Wow!*

This is the same hardheaded attitude that motivated Daniel to pay no attention to the ungodly laws of Babylon and to keep moving courageously forward, regardless of persecution.

LIVING AMONG LYONS

Iron sharpens iron (Proverbs 27:17). Marshmallows don't sharpen marshmallows. As we have soft hearts and hard heads, our ideas *will* clash with others. Yet this impact will make us sharper. And if these clashes are motivated by love, then we should embrace them, not avoid them.

Often before we battle the culture's ideas, God allows us to practice with other Christians. These types of exchanges can be part of a strengthening and maturing process. They sharpen and strengthen us for the real battles in a way nothing else can.

We enjoy this dynamic with our good friend Gabe Lyons, the founder of Q Ideas. He is also the coauthor of *unChristian* and *Good Faith*. We went to college with Gabe, and he was in both our weddings. He's one of our best friends.[2]

Here is an interesting side story about Gabe: In college he was dancing at a party—we're talking bite the bottom lip and kick out the elbows—when he suddenly just disappeared. We darted into the crowd to look for him, only to find Gabe on his back in the middle of the dance floor holding his leg. He sprained his ankle gettin' down. Classic! We actually had to carry him away. (We've been waiting almost twenty years to tell that story!)

Back to the real reason we bring up Gabe. We love him like a brother, and he loves us. And sometimes we wrestle with one another's ideas with clashing swords and butting heads. There are times he's right, times we're right, times when none of us are right, and rarely times when all of us are right!

So, as friends, we have a decision to make. Do we avoid topics where we disagree? Or do we clash swords, knowing that when the sparks fly, we *all* get sharper?

In fact, we have a few choices:

- If we have *soft* hearts and *soft* heads, we would never talk about anything that could lead us to disagree. We would just chill as buddies and talk about sports, the weather, or other safe, superficial topics. The result? A shallow friendship.
- If we have *hard* hearts and *hard* heads, we would argue

about everything and not care about the way we affect one
another. The result? A broken friendship.

+ If we have *hard* hearts and *soft* heads, then much of
our relationship would turn into negative gossip, not
caring about God or others. We might even start getting
bitter toward each other. Again, the result is a broken
friendship.

+ But if we have *soft* hearts and *hard* heads, we engage
each other with love, allow our ideas to clash for mutual
sharpening, and then top it off at the table enjoying sushi
with our wives. We would duke it out and then chill out.
(And then pig out.) The result becomes a deep and lasting
friendship.

UNCOMPROMISING AND UNCONDITIONAL

So here are our options as Christians in a world where Babylon's
ideas will clash with ours:

Option 1: HIDE
  Do what a few Christian leaders have asked us to
  do—back out of the battle altogether and only focus
  on personal purity. But this alone is not the endgame.
  Advancing God's kingdom is our mission and destiny.
  Daniel lived courageously in his journey, and so can we.
  But we cannot back out of the battle.
Option 2: RAGE
  Rage against the machine and become issue

fighters—seeking more to win debates than minister to people. Try to convert as many people to our way of thinking as possible. This option is not viable for a biblical Christian either.

Option 3: ENGAGE

Engage the culture with a soft heart and a hard head. This is what genuine biblical love looks like, what Daniel teaches us to do, and what makes us relevant to the culture from God's perspective.

Jesus gave us a great example in how He dealt with a wealthy young official. The rich young ruler asked Jesus how he could "inherit eternal life" (Mark 10:17–22). Jesus told him to keep the commandments. The man responded that he did. Then the gospel tells us that Jesus "felt love" for the man. Jesus cared deeply for him and spoke to him with compassion. But the foundation of His compassionate message was a hardheaded commitment to truth.

Jesus told the young man the one thing he did not *want* to hear but knew he *needed* to hear: He told him to give everything away and follow Him (v. 21).

Check this out in verse 22: "Disheartened by the saying, he went away sorrowful" (ESV). Wait a second! Christ's love for this man actually "disheartened" him—it ripped his heart out. And Jesus just let him walk away. He didn't chase him down to explain.

Jesus not only felt love but also showed love by inviting the man into the greatest privilege on the planet—to be His disciple. But His head was hard because He had to address the idea that kept this man from knowing the truth—the one that stood in the way of his full surrender. The man's possessions ruled him, but Jesus required unconditional love with no compromise.

That's what a soft heart and a hard head looks like in real life. Jesus loved the man but challenged and confronted his false idea of God's kingdom.

This may cost us our reputation or some friendships, but speaking "the truth in love" is our only option to bring true transformation to a culture that desperately needs both (Ephesians 4:15).

 Courageous transformers confront culture with hard heads because with soft hearts they love the people in it.

The beauty of this combination is that you have the perfect mix of tenderness with a warrior spirit, thus making a tender warrior. This is what Daniel was, and this is what we can be as well.

If we're going to live courageously and transform our world, the key is to have a hard head and a soft heart. And we're going to need it too, especially when we let the world know "there is a God in heaven" (Daniel 2:28)!

CHAPTER 13

LET IT BE KNOWN

"Today let it be known that You are God . . . and that I am Your servant."

—1 KINGS 18:36

 If you want to live courageously for God, you must *let it be known* you are fully committed to Him.

WITH A SOFT HEART toward people and a hard head toward sin, the next step is to stand courageously and *let it be known* the Lord is God and you are His servant.

God is calling modern Christians out of hiding. We are heralds of truth, declaring God's Word on the ideological battlefield of our culture. There is far too much at stake to stand down when pressured to conform or capitulate. We must let it be known that Jesus is Lord and His ways are best.

During an interview on *Fox & Friends*, we were asked, "So you guys were fired for having an opinion?" I (Jason) responded,

"We weren't fired for *having* an opinion; we were fired for *voicing* an opinion."[1]

Daniel's three buddies—Shadrach, Meshach, and Abed-nego—provide us with a lasting example of courage. They went "beast mode" to stand for righteousness, refusing to bow to Nebuchadnezzar's image (Daniel 3).

They had government jobs in a pagan nation. They served with excellence among people steeped in idolatry. Yet their conviction and commitment would never allow them to bow to any god but their own. At some point there had to be a clash. And the clash created an opportunity to turn commitment to courage—and transform the world.

King Nebuchadnezzar provided this exact scenario. Daniel 3 tells the story of how, though God revealed to the king that heaven's kingdom presided over Babylon, the king's pride gave him short-term memory loss. Instead of being humble, he made a giant image of himself. Then he demanded that everyone worship the statue.

Game on!

Construction of the massive statue occurred on a large plain in full public view. Quite possibly the king had the furnace built at the same time, but no one knows for sure. If so, that would mean as the image of worship went up, so did the chamber for punishing those who refused to bow. Either way, the king's message was clear.

Shadrach, Meshach, and Abed-nego watched this very public construction. They must have known a clash was coming with severe consequences for those who refused to bow. Their strategy was simple but costly. They would swing for the fences.

The time came for the king's dark, pagan worship service.

He gathered all of his officials from the provinces of Babylon and issued the orders. When the music played, everyone was to fall and worship the image (vv. 4–5).

Side note: We think it's interesting the way the king used music to advance his agenda. The same thing has been happening in our culture for decades. So much of our music, beginning in the 1960s, pushes an agenda of immorality and irresponsibility.

But here's where the story gets a little crazy. When the music started to play, every forehead among the vast crowd of officials touched the ground.

Except for three.

Shadrach, Meshach, and Abed-nego stood upright. Picture that for a moment. Prostrate Babylonian leaders littered the ground. But three Jewish exiles remained standing, worshipping the living God and transforming their world.

Although these three faithful guys were willing to *stand* in front of the idol, they refused to *bow* before it. They stood for everyone to see, out in public for their God, in defiance of official commands to deny Him. They had made their decision long before this moment arrived.

But why did these men even attend this service if they knew what was going to happen?

To answer this question we turn to Matthew Henry, whose Bible commentaries we have been reading for years:

> It was strange that Shadrach, Meshach, and Abed-nego, would be present at this assembly, when, it is likely, they knew for what intent it was called together. Daniel, we may suppose, was absent, either his business calling him away or having leave from the king to withdraw, unless we suppose that he

stood so high in the king's favour that none durst complain of him for his noncompliance. But why did not his companions keep out of the way? Surely because they would obey the king's orders as far as they could, and would be ready to bear a public testimony against this gross idolatry. They did not think it enough not to bow down to the image, but, being in office, thought themselves obliged to stand up against it.[2]

Boom! As leaders representing the true King, they were "obliged to stand up against it." These guys knew what faithfulness looked like in this moment. They would have to stand publicly and courageously against the king's proclamation.

Usually when we read this story, we emphasize how these dudes refused to bow. But we don't often emphasize the courageous strategy *behind* their refusal. They attended the king's worship service purposely to glorify their God. These men came to play ball—to put their conviction and commitment to work and swing for the fences. Let's spell it out:

THEY SHOWED UP.
THEY STOOD STRONG.
THEY STAYED PUT.

When the king summoned the nation's officials before the golden image, Shadrach, Meshach, and Abed-nego could have expressed their conviction and commitment without courage simply by staying at home. But they *showed up.*

Then when the herald made his announcement and the music played, the three men *stood strong* against the king's order.

And finally, when everyone else bowed (possibly including

some fellow Jewish exiles), they *stayed put*—on their feet for all to see. Courage on display.

They understood the consequences. The blazing heat of the furnace burned for any who would disobey. But these three young men stepped up to the plate, ready to swing away.

 For our courage to be displayed, we must show up, stand strong, and stay put!

As with any faithful follower of God, Shadrach, Meshach, and Abed-nego had plenty of enemies desperate for their demise. A certain group of people within the intellectual community of Babylon—the Chaldeans—told the king about their refusal to bow. They couldn't wait to see how the king would respond. (*David: This reminds us of activist groups in America today, filling our courts with lawsuits against faithful followers of Christ.*)

The king's pride took a hit when he heard they wouldn't bow, so he was enraged and asked the three if they properly understood the punishment. He challenged them by saying, "And what god is there who can deliver you out of my hands?" (Daniel 3:15).

The guys stepped up to the challenge and replied with what amounted to a full-on slap to the face, which contains our theme for this chapter:

> Shadrach, Meshach and Abed-nego replied to the king, "O Nebuchadnezzar, we do not need to give you an answer concerning this matter. If it be so, our God whom we serve is able to deliver us from the furnace of blazing fire; and He will deliver us out of your hand, O king. But even if He does not,

let it be known to you, O king, that we are not going to serve your gods or worship the golden image that you have set up."

—vv. 16–18

Holy smokes! They just horsewhipped the king of Babylon! And they let all in attendance know their God was *the* living God. They would bow before no other. They *stood* with courage and then *spoke* with courage. The two went hand in hand. Walk before talk.

They didn't even address him with the typical "O King live forever" greeting. They just called him plain ol' Nebuchadnezzar. He knew they publicly slapped his face, and they knew he would publicly slap them back. With conviction and commitment already on their side, they had all the courage they needed to stand strong as God's men.

And here's another interesting aspect of this story. The three Jews did not focus on what would happen to them. Their concern was not their fate. Their focus was God's glory in Babylon. As they told the king, even if God chose not to deliver them from the fire, they would not serve his gods or worship the golden image.

Shadrach, Meshach, and Abed-nego weren't into deal-making with God. They did not say, "God, if You save us out of this, we'll serve You." No. They were willing to do what was right without any promise that He would save them. Daniel and his friends would never adhere to today's common theology that "God just wants to make you happy, healthy, and wealthy." Their universe was not me-centered but God-centered.

 The resolve to stand is our responsibility; the result of our stand is God's.

So the king threw them into the furnace. But just as a chocolate chip doesn't lose its form in the oven, these young men kept both their spiritual *and* physical forms intact. God didn't allow them to be touched—not even the smell of smoke was on them (v. 27).

They obeyed the heart of their heavenly Father, and He chose to hook His boys up. But even if He didn't, they would have *let it be known* anyway. Now that's courage!

They publicly defied the king's command and declared their loyalty to God. This was more than civil disobedience by refusing to submit. This was biblical obedience by resolving to stand. Biblical obedience is not simply the refusal to submit to the government but the readiness to stand for God. As Peter and the apostles put it, "We must obey God rather than men" (Acts 5:29).

When the king called them out of the furnace and saw that the flame did not touch them, he was a different man (at least for a little while). He changed the law of the land to forbid people from speaking "anything offensive against the God of Shadrach, Meshach and Abed-nego," and just like that, the culture transformed in a positive direction (Daniel 3:29).

This is what faithfulness looked like for these three God-fearing public officials with influence in their city. They knew the applause of their earthly king meant nothing without the smile of their heavenly King.

KEEP WALKIN' BUT START TALKIN'

Claiming to be a person of faith is easy in today's culture. But it's quite another matter to talk about the object of your faith—to *let it be known* you won't bow to any other.

People often ask us how to positively engage the culture. Our initial response is the theme of our previous chapter: combining a soft heart with a hard head. Then we tell them simply to join the conversation. Don't stay silent or back out because you're scared of a hostile response, getting labeled a bigot, or losing your job. Let God's truth be known. Transforming faith will not come to those around us unless we speak. "So faith comes from hearing, and hearing by the word of Christ" (Romans 10:17).

This doesn't make us "issue fighters," but kingdom advancers. In other words, our goal is not to debate issues as much as it is to let it be known that Jesus is Lord and God's ways are best. Divine purpose drives our calling.

There are issues—golden images—set up throughout our culture (abortion, redefined marriage, evolution, and so forth), and the powers of darkness insist that everyone bow to them. But we cannot, and we will not. We will let it be known that whether or not we are persecuted, we will not serve their gods or worship their images. For people of courage, hot-button issues become opportunities to stand for the gospel—even if everyone else bows down. That's what transforms our world.

 We are not issue fighters but kingdom advancers. Divine purpose drives our passion.

As Abraham Kuyper once said, "When principles that run against your deepest convictions begin to win the day, then battle is your calling, and peace has become sin; you must, at the price of dearest peace, lay your convictions bare before friend and enemy, with all the fire of your faith."[3]

Courage like this is nothing new to the historical church and was certainly not new to Shadrach, Meshach, and Abed-nego. They knew the Scriptures. They were well aware of Joshua, Gideon, and David. They read the prophets. It's no coincidence that Daniel's three friends used the same words as Elijah when he stood alone against King Ahab and the prophets of Baal. Elijah prayed: "O LORD, the God of Abraham, Isaac and Israel, today *let it be known* that You are God in Israel and that I am Your servant and I have done all these things at Your word" (1 Kings 18:36).

Elijah declared "Let it be known" to a wicked king, the false prophets, and a backsliding nation that Israel's God was the only God. Likewise, Daniel's friends let Babylon know their God was the true God and King of all nations.

SERMON ON THE MOUND

I (Jason) remember an opportunity I had to let it be known when playing in my second year of professional baseball with the Frederick Keys, the class-A minor league team for the Baltimore Orioles.

Lots of kids attended the ballpark with their parents for Student Night. The place was packed. Just before the game, one of the marketing assistants came up to me and said the front office wanted me to address the crowd before the game. I was relieved they didn't ask me to sing the national anthem. That would have been a night no one would forget!

They wanted me to encourage the young people to work hard at reading and studying. Sounded good to me. Then she said, "You won't have enough time to preach a sermon or anything.

Ha! Ha!" Funny, they thought I would preach just because I was a Christian.

Right there I had a decision to make. Stand in front of everyone and give a little popcorn speech on the value of reading books and studying—a message everyone would soon forget—or let it be known that Jesus was Lord of my life—the message no one can forget. I knew I didn't have enough time to share the full gospel, only about sixty seconds.

I asked God for wisdom.

As I walked out of the clubhouse, I still didn't know what to say. But God gave me the words just before I grabbed the microphone.

The crowd of five thousand grew silent when I walked toward home plate. I was nervous, but I remember Dad always told me, "Don't let the butterflies in your stomach keep you from doing what's right. Make them fly in formation!"

I took a deep breath . . . and belted out the theme song from *The Phantom of the Opera*.

Only kidding. Just wanted to make sure you were paying attention.

I looked over the crowd and began, "I've heard it said that the most important things in life are the people you meet and the books you read. Well, I'm here to tell you that the best book I've ever read is the Holy Bible and the best person I've ever met is Jesus Christ. He's changed my life, and He'll change yours, too, if you'll commit to studying His book."

The crowd erupted in applause. People were whistling, and parents were yelling, "Way to go!" There must have been a few Christian schools there because their reactions were as if they were saying, "Finally! Someone just *said* it!"

There were plenty of people who didn't clap, but they didn't bother me. I knew I had the smile of heaven. God gave me the boldness to say it—to let it be known who my God was.

That same marketing assistant approached me later. But before she could say anything, I said, "I didn't make anybody in the front office mad, did I? I just couldn't let that opportunity pass." She said, "Actually, no. Everyone loved it. Good job." (*Phew*. Wipe the forehead.)

God allowed me to let it be known through my words that day. For the newer players on my team, that was the first time they had heard me verbalize my faith. They had seen my ways, but that night they also got to hear my words.

There were plenty of other times I failed to speak boldly for my faith. But that night became a powerful reminder that now, more than ever, is the time to let it be known that Jesus is King.

> Therefore everyone who confesses Me before men, I will also confess him before My Father who is in heaven. But whoever denies Me before men, I will also deny him before My Father who is in heaven.
>
> —MATTHEW 10:32–33

A COURAGEOUS COMPLIMENT

In the years following Christ's death, Peter and the disciples showed incredible strength and solidarity to proclaim the good news of God's kingdom to their world. But in return they experienced intense resistance from the religious leaders.

The leaders arrested Peter and John for preaching the gospel;

they threatened them and insisted they stop preaching about Jesus. But check out Peter's response:

> "Rulers of the people and elders, if we are being examined today concerning a good deed done to a crippled man, by what means this man has been healed, *let it be known* to all of you and to all the people of Israel that by the name of Jesus Christ of Nazareth, whom you crucified, whom God raised from the dead—by him this man is standing before you well."
>
> —ACTS 4:8–10 ESV

Such boldness wasn't new to the rulers, elders, and scribes. They had seen this courage before but only in one other man: Jesus Himself. Now they could tell that these men "had been with Jesus" (v. 13 ESV).

Can you imagine a greater compliment than someone recognizing you've been with Jesus? Many people long for an encounter with the one true God, and they will have one, if we have the courage to let it be known He is King—whatever the cost.

CHAPTER 14

KEEP THE WINDOWS OPEN

Now when Daniel knew that the document was signed, he entered his house (now in his roof chamber he had windows open toward Jerusalem); and he continued kneeling on his knees three times a day, praying and giving thanks before his God, as he had been doing previously.

—DANIEL 6:10

 If everything around you changes, everything inside you shouldn't!

SHADRACH, MESHACH, AND ABED-NEGO faced the fire inside the furnace. Daniel felt the lions' breath on his face in the den. All four men made their stand publicly, courageously placing their private convictions and commitments on full display for all to see.

There comes a time in all of our lives when, after we have lived with conviction and commitment privately, the Spirit of God will call on us to stand with courage publicly.

The cultural campaign today is to privatize our Christian faith—"just keep it to yourself." Yet courageous champions, such as Daniel and his friends, kept it public. And so should we.

Shadrach, Meshach, and Abed-nego were commanded to bow, but they "let it be known" that God was their true King and they would bow to no other (Daniel 3). Daniel was commanded *not* to bow; remember, there was a law in the land stating no one was to pray to anyone but the king (Daniel 6:6–7). But in our opening verse for this chapter, we discover that he kept his windows open, kneeling before the one God and King, even after the law forbade his prayers. Both were public professions of faith requiring supernatural courage—a courage that transformed their world.

By keeping his windows open toward Jerusalem, we believe Daniel demonstrated that he didn't care who saw him—his neighbors, the administrators, or anyone else. He was going to pray no matter what, courageously defying the king's command. This story reveals how we, as followers of God, must refuse to compromise who we are, even when the culture and the governing laws are changed to target our faith. When everything around Daniel changed, he didn't. It's that simple.

Here's how the scene went down in Daniel 6. When Darius the Mede became king, he appointed Daniel as one of his top three administrators. The other leaders in the kingdom answered to these administrators. But in time, Daniel distinguished himself above the other two. His commitment to excellence, coupled with God's divine favor, couldn't be matched. And everyone took notice. So soon after taking the throne, the king planned to place the entire kingdom under Daniel's control. This didn't go over well with the other leaders, so they came up with a plan to get rid of him.

Daniel lived and worked above reproach. The officials knew they could not accuse him of doing something *wrong*. So they tried to indict him for doing something *right*. If they could twist Daniel's public loyalty to God into something criminal, then they would bring him down. So they manipulated the king to create a new injunction. Anyone who petitioned a god or man besides the king for thirty days would be cast into a den of lions.

 If persecutors can't get you to bow to *their* god, they'll try to force you not to bow to yours.

The administrators advised the king to establish this injunction "according to the law of the Medes and Persians" (v. 8). This was a crucial part of their plan. These men knew the law well. The Medes and Persians were so enamored with their own wisdom that they had created a law that stated any injunction made by the king could not be revoked, even by the king himself. This was the same type of law King Ahasuerus made to destroy the Jews during Esther's time, when Haman targeted Mordecai's courageous faith (Esther 3 and 8).

Daniel knew exactly what this would mean. No matter how much favor he had with Darius, there was no way the king could save him.

As you've read, this was Daniel's response:

Now when Daniel knew that the document was signed, he entered his house (now in his roof chamber he had windows open toward Jerusalem); and he continued kneeling on his knees three times a day, praying and giving thanks before his God, as he had been doing previously.

—DANIEL 6:10

Daniel knew the decree was signed into irrevocable law. But still he went to his room and continued his custom of praying to God with the windows open toward Jerusalem. He changed nothing.

 Laws may threaten our liberty but never our love for the Lord.

Why would Daniel have a custom of praying three times a day in his room with the windows open toward Jerusalem? He knew God's promise:

> When Your people go out to battle against their enemy, by whatever way You shall send them, *and they pray to the* LORD *toward the city which You have chosen and the house which I have built for Your name*, then hear in heaven their prayer and their supplication, and maintain their cause.
>
> —1 KINGS 8:44–45

When the culture around him no longer favored Daniel's commitments—and actually targeted his faith—he stood with courage. Daniel's conviction to live for God was far greater than his persecutors' commitment to kill him.

Why didn't Daniel just go to his bedroom and pray toward Jerusalem with his windows shut? Why not live another day so he could have more impact for God in Babylon? Thirty days isn't *that* long, so why not just pray privately until the injunction was lifted? Then when the law was revoked, Daniel could have simply advised the king not to allow such an injunction to ever pass again.

Shutting the windows could have been a really relevant move on Daniel's part. He probably would have won the approval of some other Jews who already prayed in private. But his reverence for God wouldn't allow him to change his practice. Though this made no strategic sense to keep the windows open, his decision made perfect spiritual sense.

Daniel did not focus on keeping the platform of influence God had given him. He focused on the presence of the One who gave it to him in the first place. He was willing to hold his platform with an open hand and face his fear, just as David had done when he defeated Goliath.

So Daniel resisted the injunction by refusing to hide, knowing his enemies were watching him closely. As soon as they saw him praying, they reported to the king, "Daniel, who is one of the exiles from Judah, pays no attention to you, O king" (Daniel 6:13).

He paid no attention to the king? Wait just a minute! His attention to the king was exactly why he was about to be promoted over the entire kingdom. This was simply a false narrative created by his persecutors. Sound familiar? Those who stand courageously today for biblical values will be *falsely* accused as well (Matthew 5:11).

But Daniel did not defend himself against this lie and accusation. Neither did he violate his conscience by obeying the unrighteous decree.

King Darius was heartsick when he heard the news, knowing the law could not be revoked. We can just hear him now: "I can't believe those liars tricked me into signing a law targeting my best leader!" Now he would have to live with the reality of his bad decision. The king tried to save Daniel, but his attempts failed (Daniel 6:14). He had no choice but to throw his top advisor to the lions.

Before the stone was rolled over the mouth of the den, the king's final words revealed how Daniel was able to stand with such courage: "Your God whom you *constantly* serve will Himself deliver you" (v. 16).

Check that out—his testimony clearly penetrated the heart of this pagan king. He was certain Daniel's God would save him. Then Darius went home and fasted (v. 18). That's not something pagan kings would normally do.

For one long night, Daniel lived among lions. At dawn the king ran to the den with a cry of anxiety: "Daniel, servant of the living God, has your God, whom you constantly serve, been able to deliver you from the lions?" (v. 20). Do you see the transformation happening here? The king clung to Daniel's faith. God had touched the heart of Darius by allowing Daniel to get into a fix that only God could fix.

Notice Daniel's response: "My God sent His angel and shut the lions' mouths and they have not harmed me, inasmuch as I was found innocent before Him; and also toward you, O king, I have committed no crime" (v. 22).

Now wait a second! Rewind. There was a law in place, and Daniel broke the law. Wasn't that a crime? Wasn't that civil disobedience? The real issue is following biblical obedience first.

Scripture clearly states we are to be subject to the governing authorities, but there is no command that government holds *absolute* authority—that belongs only to God. So if government, as a "minister of God," begins to do evil, we have the obligation to resist—to reset the principle to God's design, where good is praised and evil is punished (Romans 13:1–7; 1 Peter 2:14).

Daniel knew when to obey God rather than the king:

1. When he was prohibited from expressing his faith (Daniel 6:10; Acts 5:29).
2. When he was forced to act against his faith (Daniel 3:12).

The key is to determine whose laws are supreme.

So King Darius removed Daniel from the lions' den without harm. Then he threw Daniel's accusers and their entire families to their doom. King Darius wanted to wipe out not only the men but also any reminders of them and their legacy. The same fate Daniel's enemies planned for him came upon them (Daniel 6:23–24).

 God's confirmation will come down when our courage rises up.

So what was the result of Daniel's faithfulness? Total transformation.

The king changed.

The law changed.

The culture was changed.

Daniel's enemies were removed.

Another stake of testimony for God's kingdom was driven deep into the heart of Babylon because of the courage of a godly man who refused to change.

COMING TO A CROSSROAD

As much as we love the example of Daniel keeping his windows open and refusing to change when the law was enacted, our favorite story of taking a stand for biblical obedience is one we witnessed ourselves.

Our dad has been a street preacher since we were kids. Although he was a pastor and had a pulpit inside the church, he felt his true platform was outside the church. So we spent many hot summer days listening to our dad deliver the good news to thousands of passersby. (*Jason: David would usually hide when Dad grabbed the microphone!*)

His preaching went to a whole nutha' level when he discovered one of the most densely populated locations in Charlotte, North Carolina. He found a restaurant that had a sidewalk conveniently located at the area's busiest intersection. Dad was mentoring a handful of "preacher boys" who would line up out there every Friday and Saturday to preach. After several months, some of the leaders in our city decided to put a stop to Dad's street ministry. So they crafted an ordinance to get him off the sidewalk (the sidewalk our taxes paid for, by the way).

They didn't want to call this an injunction because they knew it wouldn't stand up in court. So they called the law a "parade ordinance," which prohibited organized gatherings of five people or more on public sidewalks. As with Daniel's story, the deceitful decree was passed.

I (David) remember the day the law was signed. Dad called me and said, "Dave, I need you to get four friends—don't forget your brother—and meet me at the intersection where I preach this Friday at 5:00 p.m."

"What's going on?" I asked.

"Our city just passed an ordinance that targets me and the other street preachers. They disguised it as a rule to prevent public gatherings without permits, but in fact it's designed to get us to stop doing what we've always done: preach God's Word publicly. The fine is five thousand dollars."

"So you want me to break the law with you?" I responded.

"No. I just need you guys to help *me* break the law because I can't do this by myself. I need four other guys! Now hang up and get to work."

Okay, I understand that most of you don't even *know* people who talk like this, let alone have a dad who does. But for me, this kind of discussion was normal. So I called Jason.

"Dude, Dad wants us to meet him on the sidewalk to break some law that was just passed. He needs our help."

"You're kidding, right?" Jason replied. "Okay, I'll be there."

I then called a few good buddies and repeated what I had told Jason. Amazingly, not one of them asked a single question. They just said, "I'll be there."

Courage is contagious. A man willing to have his "windows open toward Jerusalem" will embolden others to do the same. For example, as Paul sat in prison for the gospel, he wrote to the church in Philippi, "Most of the brethren, trusting in the Lord because of my imprisonment, have far more courage to speak the word of God without fear" (Philippians 1:14).

So we showed up at 5:00 p.m., and Dad was already out there preaching. When he saw us, he put the microphone down and came over to give us the plan.

"I already told the police I'm going to break the injunction. They should be on their way. So when they get here, I need you guys to stand shoulder to shoulder right next to me. They're going to warn you, and then you can walk away. But when they get to me, I'm going to refuse to leave and break the law. Then I'm going to refuse to pay the fine. Then we'll end up in court. Then I'm going to win, and we'll continue to have the freedom to preach in the streets!"

I kid you not. This is exactly how our dad talked—and still does to this day.

We took our positions as the police arrived. (*I'm sure I saw Jason's knees knocking.*) As we stood there waiting for them to issue our warnings, Dad started preaching again.

I was the first one to go, then Jason, and then one of our buddies. But when the officers got to two of our friends, Jason Dellinger and Scott Heldreth, they refused to leave. It was an amazing sight. They weren't about to walk away. (Apparently, we didn't have the same courage.) After writing their tickets, the officers then got to Dad. He politely stopped to listen to them for a minute and then went right back to preaching.

Even as I write this, I feel the courage of these men in my bones!

All three received fines, and all of them refused to pay. Dad called his attorney and told him what happened. Within a few days the city received a letter that basically dropped legal hay-makers on them. They immediately withdrew the fines and repealed the ordinance.

Dad told us later he wasn't as concerned about his rights as he was his responsibility to *do* what was right. Like Daniel and his friends, he stood tall and opened his windows with courage.

Even when our rights are not recognized, we have a responsibility to do what's right.

Dad had a custom of preaching God's Word every Friday at 5:00 p.m., and he wasn't about to change just because the laws and culture around him did. This ordinance targeted God's people and was abolished by God's people. Why? Dad refused to change—he kept his windows open.

DELLY'S DANIEL DECISION

So what do you do when the culture around you changes? What will you do? That day is already here, so you need to decide what your response will be when the laws no longer favor your religious liberty. Will you remain unchanged when the accusers turn on *you*?

Not everyone will be put in a position to stand against a king as Daniel and his buddies were or will find himself or herself publicly challenging a city ordinance as our dad did. But everyone can be courageous by refusing to change who he or she is. Everyone can keep his or her windows open.

One of our friends from the previous story, Jason Dellinger (Delly), is a living example of this kind of courage. We played baseball together at Liberty, so we've known him for a long time. His voicemail greeting has always ended with "Jesus loves you." This was a custom he had built into his life. But this was challenged the day his employer told him to remove the name of Jesus from the voicemail. If he refused, he would be fired.

He could have changed the message to "God bless you." But he knew a greater truth was at stake. For him, this would have been paramount to shutting his windows. Delly saw this as a deliberate attack to silence his Christian faith. So he refused to change his words.

And he got fired. (Actually, they forced him to resign, and he did so respectfully.)

For the next two years Delly worked cleaning houses, mowing lawns, and any other odd jobs he could find. He had to provide for his wife and three small kids. Every time we saw him at our properties working, we were inspired by his courage to keep his windows open and remain unchanged in a post-Christian culture.

Delly now has *six* kids and continues to sell insurance for another company as a successful agent. He also travels and speaks with us from time to time, encouraging Christians to stand boldly for their faith.

YOUR TURN

We've looked in detail at stories of courage about Daniel, his friends, and our friends. But our deepest prayer and intent for this book is for you to display courage, for you to transform your world. Through Jesus Christ, we have the power inside us to do just that. But this takes courage to release that power, courage that keeps the windows open when it would be easier just to close them and live to fight another day.

Daniel's story was not written simply for a Bible school lesson, but for God's people in *any* Babylon. God has handed us His instructions on how to have courage to stand when everyone else is bowing. Let's be Daniels, entrusting ourselves to God and leaving the results to Him.

The Enemy of our souls will try to scare us with the threat of lions, or he may try to lure us away by buying us off. So as we'll see in the next chapter, we must always stand with courage and never allow ourselves to be bought at any price.

CHAPTER 15

"KEEP YOUR GIFTS"

Then Daniel answered and said before the king, "Keep your gifts for yourself or give your rewards to someone else."

—DANIEL 5:17

 If you can be bought, there will always be a buyer.

DANIEL'S FRIENDS *LET IT be known* that the God of heaven was their King. Daniel himself *kept his windows open* and prayed in defiance of a king's decree. Later in his life, Daniel *refused the king's gifts* because his faithfulness to God didn't have a price. He refused to be bought.

By *gifts*, we mean the goodies of the world that stand in the way of the greatness of God's kingdom. They come in any form of fame, fortune, or promotion promised by getting along with the world.

Daniel's life didn't have a price tag. His services weren't for sale. No amount of worldly gifts or kingly accolades could deter him from his mission. He was a man of deep conviction, dedicated commitment, and undeniable courage; the grace of heaven was far more important to him than the gifts of men.

Keeping our gaze on the grace of heaven keeps our grip off the gifts of men.

Daniel's life provides a fresh look at this truth. And this challenge gives us all a moment to pause and ask ourselves these questions: *Can I be bought? What would it take to silence my faith? To cower from my convictions? To keep my relationship with God private? Is it a six-figure salary? A major promotion? Elected office? Celebrity status? Growing church membership? The promise of keeping my platform?*

The moment we grab the goodies of the world, we give up the greatness of the kingdom.

In *Whatever the Cost* we explained how Satan tries to move us off the track of God's mission by either scaring us or luring us. On the one hand, he uses fear and intimidation to back us down and keep us quiet. On the other hand, he tries to lure us away with our own dreams, desires, passions, goals, and even gifts, if he can find our price to sell out. If the Devil can keep our hands full of gifts from the world, we won't have a hand free to pick up the sword of the Spirit. So let's get personal. Ask yourself the question, and be intentional with your answer: *Can I be bought?*

The Bible has something to say about this:

For what does it profit a man to gain the whole world, and forfeit his soul? (Mark 8:36)

Their minds are corrupt, and they have turned their backs on the truth. To them, a show of godliness is just a way to become wealthy. (1 Timothy 6:5 NLT)

KING B AND THE BUTT KICKIN'

There was a new king in town. Belshazzar had taken over the throne from his forefather, Nebuchadnezzar. (You gotta love all those crazy Bible names.) We'll call Belshazzar King B for short. Here's what went down in Daniel 5.

King B was a bad man, filled with pride and basking in the glory of Babylon. He forgot how God humbled Nebuchadnezzar by making him eat grass and live like an animal for seven years (Daniel 4:33). But that's how pride can blind us.

One evening, King B defied the God of heaven. As he partied with a thousand of his nobles, he decided to let everyone drink from the vessels of gold and silver taken from the Lord's temple.

Stop there. He knew the temple and its articles were sacred, representing the presence of the God of Israel. So he basically spit in the face of Daniel's faith. This never ends well.

As the king and his friends were partying and praising the gods of gold and silver, a human hand appeared, writing on the wall in front of them all. *Uh, check please!* We're sure that's a party nobody forgot.

The king's face went fifty shades of white. His knees started knocking together (even though the Macarena didn't exist yet). He called for all the wise men in Babylon to come and interpret the writing. He promised a purple robe, a gold chain, and the third position in the kingdom to anyone who could read and interpret the message. (Again, his youthful arrogance blinded him to the fact that Nebuchadnezzar would've just called for Daniel.)

But all these gifts—what a great offer! The wise men tried the best they could. Yet nothing. No clue. No robe. No chain. No position.

God's message requires God's messenger.

The king's wife reminded him about Daniel and how he interpreted dreams for King Nebuchadnezzar. So he summoned God's man.

As usual, Daniel was a game changer. The moment he entered the scene, as we mentioned in our discussion on purity in chapter 11, God's clarity dispelled the confusion. And the way he spoke to the king was more like the way someone would speak to a rebel. This man had just spit in the face of the living God and Daniel would receive nothing from him: "Keep your gifts for yourself or give your rewards to someone else; however, I will read the inscription to the king and make the interpretation known to him" (Daniel 5:17).

Oh no, he didn't! Refusing a gift from the king was not something people did back then. This was a bold move on Daniel's part, letting everyone know his services weren't for sale.

This response was rock solid. Daniel essentially said he didn't need the promise of payment to do his duty and wouldn't be bought. He was a prophet, not a professional. God sent him there to deliver His message. That was his sole reason for being there. This wasn't a time to receive gifts, especially from a king defying heaven. Daniel needed both hands to wield the sword of the Spirit he was about to unsheathe: the Word of God.

Here's what happened. Before Daniel read the inscription, he dropped a haymaker on the king with a history lesson on humility. First he declared God's sovereignty over all things, including Babylon. Then he recounted Nebuchadnezzar's pride and how God humbled him years before King B was born. He finished the lesson with a straight-up rebuke: "Yet you, his son, Belshazzar, have not humbled your heart, even though you knew all this" (v. 22).

Daniel was only supposed to interpret the message. Instead, like any good elder, he gave the king a lecture on youthful pride. Then he rebuked him. That is what courage that cannot be bought looks like.

The king's reaction didn't matter to Daniel; he looked for the reward of his heavenly King. This gave him the courage to say what needed to be said.

 Focusing on the reward of heaven's King brings the courage to speak truth to earth's kings.

So Daniel interpreted God's message (paraphrasing verses 26 and 27 here): "Your time on the top has come to an end, big boy! You're full of yourself and pretty much hollow. So I've decided to give everything you have over to another nation." Ouch.

Even though Daniel had refused the king's gifts, the king gave them to him anyway. Interesting.

That same night the message became a reality. King B was slain, and a new king sat on the throne of Babylon, right after a proclamation circulated that Daniel was now third in command over the kingdom. How incredible is that? God divinely orchestrated the promotion of Daniel just moments before a massive kingdom shift took place.

Daniel's world transformed yet again because he had the courage to resist the gifts of the world and speak the truth. He could not be bought. Yet God gave him all the gifts anyway. *Boom!*

DOLLARS AND SENSE

Several years ago Dad received a phone call from a man who wanted to support his pro-life ministry. Calls like this one were always a miracle because Dad never asked for money. So when he received this call, we got excited.

The man said he would write Dad a check for thirty thousand dollars. *Snap!* He had always lived day-to-day as a vocational minister, so this was a *huge* answer to our prayers. But then Dad started asking some questions and discovered the man had just won the money from the state lottery. Now he wanted to give a tithe (10 percent) toward a pro-life ministry. Dad politely thanked the man but explained he could not take the money. The potential donor could keep his gift.

You probably think Dad is a crazy man. That's okay because we did too. Whether you agree or not isn't the point. The *reason* Dad refused the money is the point.

When he told us he turned the man down, we jumped all over him.

"Dad! Are you serious? This money could be used for so much good! Who cares that you disagree with the lottery and preach against it? Call the dude back and let him know you'll take it!"

"Boys, I don't care whether you disagree with me. The fact remains that the lottery hurts poor people. They take their hard-earned money and spend it on a 'wish' for riches. That's not God's best for them. Work is God's best for them—it's a win-win. The lottery is a win-lose. I preach against this, and I refuse to bend my convictions for thirty thousand dollars. The gospel can't be bought."

As we watched Dad drive off in his beat-up blue Suburban with 250,000 miles on it and head back to his eleven-hundred-square-foot house, we both sat in amazement. Now *that's* a man of conviction who cannot be bought.

When the reality TV money started coming at us, we remembered this story. We didn't want to forget the point like Belshazzar did. So right out of the gate, as different networks began offering us shows, we said: "We are Christians, and no amount of fame or fortune will deter us from that fact. We will not wear 'golden handcuffs' just so we can become rich and famous."

PROPHETS, PARADES, AND PRICE TAGS

Once again we ask the crucial questions: Can you be bought? What would it take?

Two men in Scripture show us two different ways of approaching the allure of gifts: Mordecai, another exile like Daniel; and Gehazi, Elisha the prophet's assistant in a story Daniel certainly knew.

Mordecai's account is great for spiritual leaders who may be tempted to focus on the praise and promotion the world has to offer in exchange for their silence on the "hot issues" of the day. He was the older cousin of Esther, a Jew who became queen of Persia. She saved the Jews from wicked Haman's plot to destroy them. Mordecai was the catalyst behind the scenes, encouraging Esther and sparking her to action.

After revealing a plot to assassinate the king, Mordecai was rewarded with great public honor. The king paraded him, wearing a royal robe and a crown, around the city on one of his own horses (Esther 6:9). This was a big deal back in the day. It would be like the president of the United States flying you around the country in Air Force One, telling everyone how amazing you are.

Can you imagine what that must have felt like for Mordecai? The king thought he was the bomb. He had it made—book deals, speaking gigs, and TV shows were comin'!

But Mordecai sought for nothing. After being honored, he got off the king's horse and went right back to his place at the gate, where he had been faithful for years (v. 12).

When you're on a mission for God, you cannot allow gifts to become a lure. Some leaders today don't want to get off Mordecai's horse. They like the royal robe and want to keep the crowds cheering. They enjoy the recognition of being escorted around the city—all for God's glory, of course—but they belong back at their gates, just like Mordecai. Getting paraded around should not be a distraction from God's mission.

 The parades of man will never match the peace of God's mission.

It's time to get off the horse. If God wants to elevate us, we need to let Him do the promotion His way, in His time. There's nothing wrong with gifts, promotions, or other blessings in and of themselves. But we must never take our eyes off God's approval and put our focus on the world's rewards.

Unlike Mordecai, Gehazi *could* be bought. His story teaches us that if we just want the gifts, we may get them. But we'll also get the burden that comes with them.

Centuries before Daniel, a well-respected and highly decorated Syrian general, Naaman, was diseased with leprosy (2 Kings 5). His king sent him to visit the prophet Elisha in Israel for healing. Naaman left for the journey with an abundance of gifts for Elisha. After following the prophet's instructions, he was healed instantly. Amazed and incredibly grateful, Naaman offered Elisha gifts fit for a king. But Elisha refused to take them. His healing wasn't for hire. He told Naaman, "I will take nothing" (v. 16).

But Gehazi, Elisha's servant, overheard the offer from Naaman and was not about to let an opportunity like this pass by. So after Naaman departed for Syria, Gehazi secretly chased him down and took the gifts for himself. His earthly mind-set, unlike Elisha's heavenly one, motivated him not only to grab at the gifts but also to ambitiously pursue them.

When Gehazi arrived back to Elisha, the prophet asked him, "Is this the time to take money or to accept clothes—or olive groves and vineyards, or flocks and herds, or male and female slaves?" (v. 26 NIV).

"Is this the time?" That's the question today as well. Is this the time to go after the gifts of the world? Is this the time to stay on the king's horse and abandon the gates?

If we don't see ourselves on God's mission for God's rewards, we'll keep chasing the gifts of man. But those will steal our hearts and sap our courage. Yes, we may receive all the world has to offer, only to realize that burdens go along with them.

Notice how Gehazi was cursed after he got all of Naaman's gifts: "Therefore, the leprosy of Naaman shall cling to you" (v. 27). Gehazi wanted the gifts, and he got them—along with the disease. Gehazi wanted Naaman's stuff, so he got *all* of Naaman's stuff.

WANTED: WARRIORS

Is this the time to seek a name for yourself? To water down the truth to keep people happy? To posture for position? To keep quiet so you stay in everyone's good graces?

Is this the time?

Gehazi didn't understand the times in which he lived. Daniel and Mordecai did. They (as did the sons of Issachar) not only understood their times, but they also knew what to do (1 Chronicles 12:32). Daniel recognized these times weren't for personal glory and worldly promotion. He had bigger fish to fry—more urgent matters to attend to. As Moses, "considering the reproach of Christ greater riches than the treasures of Egypt . . . he was looking to the reward" (Hebrews 11:26). The real reward, that is: God Himself.

The marines may be looking for a few good men, but God is simply looking for those who can't be bought. He's looking for those "whose hearts are completely His," who would never sell out, who aren't motivated nor deterred by what the world has to offer (2 Chronicles 16:9 HCSB).

CHAPTER 16

SEEK THE WELFARE OF THE CITY

Seek the welfare of the city where I have sent you into exile, and pray to the LORD on its behalf; for in its welfare you will have welfare.

—JEREMIAH 29:7

 When love motivates your heart, blessing your city becomes as basic to life as blinking.

WHEN ANOTHER NATION CONQUERS your hometown, destroys your temple, and carries you and your people away into exile, you might feel you have good reason to be bitter and angry. You might want to "rage against the machine"—pointing your finger and righteously standing against that evil nation. These things happened to Daniel, but he was a man of a different spirit. Correctly stated, a *very* different Spirit.

So what did Daniel do in his new city? He didn't seek the

welfare *from* his city—he sought the welfare *of* his city. He did not merely identify its problems; he sought powerful solutions.

 The courage that transforms a nation seeks to bless the nation even when people refuse that blessing.

Daniel had the reputation of a life of service and excellence as a top official. His whole life was dedicated to Babylon's well-being. Add to that his supernatural ministry, and he brought great value to Babylon.

Service was Daniel's mind-set, which revealed his courageous commitment to God's Word as we mentioned in our discussion in chapter 8. The Lord had spoken through the prophet Jeremiah to the exiles and told them how to conduct themselves in this new land:

> "Thus says the LORD of hosts, the God of Israel, to all the exiles whom I have sent into exile from Jerusalem to Babylon, 'Build houses and live in them; and plant gardens and eat their produce. Take wives and become the fathers of sons and daughters, and take wives for your sons and give your daughters to husbands, that they may bear sons and daughters; and multiply there and do not decrease. Seek the welfare of the city where I have sent you into exile, and pray to the LORD on its behalf; for in its welfare you will have welfare.'"
>
> —JEREMIAH 29:4–7

Daniel obeyed this command.

God did not call His people to sit back and ignore the needs

SEEK THE WELFARE OF THE CITY

of their city out of resentment. He did not send them to complain about and critique Babylon, even though this nation was destroying their homeland. God did not want His people to separate themselves into a holy huddle and talk about the good ol' days back in Jerusalem. Nor were they to plan a coup or massive escape. The prophetic Word instructed them to stay put and seek the welfare of their new city. How's that for a game-changing paradigm?

God called His people to be lightning bolts, not lightning bugs. They were to be a part of the solution, not a part of the problem. They were to bring value to their city, not simply receive value from it.

In my (David's) first year in major league spring training with the St. Louis Cardinals, I learned a valuable lesson from our catching coach. He had played with all of the St. Louis greats—Bob Gibson, Lou Brock, Stan Musial, and others. So all the catchers clung to his every word.

After one practice he called us together and said, "Let me tell you something, fellas. Don't ever criticize or critique anyone unless you're willing to help. I get on you boys every day like a bat out of hell, but I'm invested in you; I care about you; I've *earned* the right to critique you."

This statement profoundly impacted me and helped shape the way I interacted with players for the rest of my professional career. Although my catching coach is no longer with us today, his legacy lives in my heart. He wanted the best for his players, and we all knew it.

What motivated my coach was the same thing that motivated

Daniel: love. Daniel really cared about the people in the country where God sent him. That is the starting point to seeking the welfare of your city.

When God warned Nebuchadnezzar in a dream that he would suffer for his pride, Daniel didn't gloat. As we learned in chapter 12, he lovingly consoled him, saying, "My lord, if only the dream applied to those who hate you and its interpretation to your adversaries!" (Daniel 4:19). If we were forced to serve a pagan king who had conquered our nation, we probably would've said something like, "Yeah! You got what's comin' to you now, sucka!" But not Daniel; the attitude of his heart was motivated by love—even for a pagan leader filled with pride. That's very convicting. Jesus said, after all, "But I say unto you, Love your enemies, bless them that curse you, do good to them that hate you, and pray for them which despitefully use you, and persecute you" (Matthew 5:44 KJV).

Daniel's love didn't stop at consolation. He proceeded to exhort the king in love to turn from his wicked ways and prosper: "Therefore, O king, may my advice be pleasing to you: break away now from your sins by doing righteousness and from your iniquities by showing mercy to the poor, in case there may be a prolonging of your prosperity" (Daniel 4:27).

Daniel genuinely cared for the king as a friend, and he offered the most helpful counsel possible. Love doesn't sit quietly by as others walk in sin to their death. Love exhorts people to turn from wickedness so they may have life.

> Righteousness exalts a nation,
> But sin is a disgrace to any people.
> —PROVERBS 14:34

Daniel desired the grace of God upon the nation, not the disgrace of sin.

Daniel sought the king's prosperity, not his harm. He wanted the king to flourish and walk in wholeness with God. He looked past his office and behavior to have compassion on the man's soul. This is the attitude that must permeate today's church if we really want to seek the welfare of *our* cities.

But love goes even further, interceding for the land and praying that everyone would come to the knowledge of God. As Paul wrote to Timothy:

> First of all, then, I urge that entreaties and prayers, petitions and thanksgivings, be made on behalf of all men, for kings and all who are in authority, so that we may lead a tranquil and quiet life in all godliness and dignity. This is good and acceptable in the sight of God our Savior, who desires all men to be saved and to come to the knowledge of the truth.
>
> —1 Timothy 2:1–4

When love motivates our hearts, blessing our city becomes as basic as blinking. We don't even have to think about it; we'll just act on the instinct.

CONDUITS AND CUL-DE-SACS

Standing on the outside of our government today and pointing the finger at our leaders is very easy. Gathering in our sacred buildings and refusing to say or do anything is even easier. But stepping in and trying to help—rolling up our sleeves and getting dirty—is much more difficult. Here's where we look to transformers like Daniel who are willing to seek the welfare of the city at their own expense.

Webster's 1828 dictionary defines *welfare* as "exemption from misfortune, sickness, calamity, or evil; the enjoyment of health and the common blessings of life, prosperity, happiness, applied to all persons."[1]

Daniel wasn't just a blessed man (with God's wisdom and favor), but he was also a blessing to men, like Abraham before him (Genesis 12:2). To *be* a blessing is a promise given to all of God's people. If those around us are not blessed, then we must ask if we have become *cul-de-sacs* instead of *conduits*. God did not intend our blessings to stop with us but to flow through us.[2]

 God designed us to be His conduits, not cul-de-sacs, with blessings flowing through us, not stopping with us.

The church today tends to be more concerned with protecting and conserving the institution of Christianity rather than going into the world to be a blessing and making disciples of the nations.

From the early church down through history, faithful followers of Christ blessed their nations by serving the broken world through the power of the Holy Spirit and God's extraordinary love. As a result, wherever Christians went, the sick, needy, and rejected were healed, cared for, and received. Marriages and families thrived, education was encouraged, and nations were blessed. People came to Christ daily because His people had the selfless attitude to be a blessing rather than consume their blessing.

The same was true in America at one time. The church was the leading builder of hospitals, schools, children's homes, community centers, and the like. Yet today, many churches spend far more time and money building and maintaining facilities for their members than blessing the citizens of their city.

According to the Evangelical Christian Credit Union, 82 percent of the average church's budget is spent on personnel, buildings, and administration expense while only 3 percent is used for children and youth programs, 2 percent for adult programs, and 1 percent on benevolence.[3]

Our good friend Dr. Bob Gladstone often asks the question, "If our churches lost their buildings, budgets, and paid staff, would we still have a church in America?" Oh boy, it's getting real now.

"Seek the welfare of the city!" The preamble to the Constitution of the United States of America states that one of the duties of government is to "promote the general welfare." It doesn't say "provide" the welfare but "promote" it. The role of the people is to provide for their own welfare while the government promotes their efforts. And for those who cannot provide for themselves, the *church* has been commissioned to step in and help.

In fact, that's the whole purpose behind tax-exempt status. Because of the church's consistent work in providing services to society, our country determined that the institution would not have to pay taxes. Practical acts of compassion from God's people have written vital parts of our nation's history.[4]

One of a church's principal roles in the world is to seek the welfare of its city. If we continue recent trends to abandon this responsibility, then there is only one institution left to fill the role—the government.

WHEN GOD'S PEOPLE GO TO WORK

As you come to realize that you *are* the church and don't just *go* to church, you'll begin to *live* like the church. As we've discussed, you must recognize that you are a minister of God—regardless of where you are placed or how you are paid. You are on a mission for Him wherever you go. Your work is a part of your worship. With this perspective, seeking the good of your city will become natural to you.

We have three good friends who recognized problems in their city and decided to seek its welfare by providing kingdom solutions—a bank employee, a stay-at-home mom, and a business owner.

Cyril Prabhu, an executive at a large bank, grieved over the issue of fatherlessness in the Carolinas. He mourned its devastating impact not only on the family but also on the economy. So he did some research. Two statistics stood out:

1. If a child's father had been to prison, it was 82 percent more likely the child would too.
2. About 85 percent of inmates grew up in a fatherless environment.[5]

Cyril realized the vicious cycle. So he asked God to give him an idea that would bless the dads and their families, lower the number of men in prison, and thus decrease the financial burden on North and South Carolina.

God spoke and answered his prayer. He would partner with churches and businesses across the Carolinas to help connect the children back to their fathers in prison and use this ministry to inspire good behavior from the inmates and in the children. Check out what he did.

In his first project he brought in truckloads of school supplies and set up a back-to-school shop in a prison chapel. The prisoners picked out backpacks full of supplies for their kids and mailed them to their children with personal notes inside, encouraging them to be good students and obey the law. Many of the kids began writing to their dads, and relationships began to strengthen. Then Cyril decided to have a reconciliation service. The families came to the prison, and the dads washed the feet of their children, apologized for their behavior, and committed to becoming good fathers—even while incarcerated.

Cyril realized even the most hardened criminals love their children and want to be good dads. They don't want their kids to spend their lives behind bars. The prisoners who participated in the back-to-school shop and reconciliation service got credit for good behavior, which was a brilliant idea. The warden at the prison reported a significant decrease in disciplinary actions. They've traced this directly back to Cyril's ministry. As of the writing of this book, Cyril now operates in ten prisons, where programs like these help make prisons safer and reduce the number of repeat offenders.

Cyril didn't just get upset about the problem. He did something about it. Today his ministry, Proverbs226, is connected to more than five thousand children. The governor of South Carolina has asked for his program to be implemented across all the prisons in the state. Other city officials are now reaching out to him to do the program in their prisons. How awesome is that?[6]

Another dear friend, Sheryl Chandler, a homeschooling mom, saw the enormous need in Charlotte, North Carolina, to help mothers who wanted to abort their babies. Many of them believed their only choice was to take their child's life. Sheryl saw the hurt and pain this decision brought to families, so she decided to do something.

She founded Truth and Mercy Pro-Life Ministries, an organization that ministers to abortion-bound mothers and provides baby showers for those who choose against abortion and allow their babies to live. Sheryl's ministry throws dozens of baby showers each year with each one representing a life saved.

We'll never forget attending our first event for four young mothers who chose life. Sheryl had the place packed with cribs, strollers, diapers, car seats, swings, clothes, and gift cards. As the moms walked in, they were stunned. There wasn't a dry eye in the room as she showered those mamas with all the Christian love she could give. And their lives were changed forever.

Since 1988, Sheryl has provided hundreds of baby showers. She still receives pictures from moms who chose life as a result of her ministry. And some of those kids are now starting families of their own! All because Sheryl sought the welfare of her city.[7]

Jim Noble, owner of the King's Kitchen restaurant in Charlotte, decided to do something about homelessness in his city. As an elite restaurateur, Jim opened a place in the heart of uptown Charlotte to give homeless people the opportunity to learn a job skill.

We remember our first meal at the King's Kitchen. The most diverse group of individuals greeted us, waited on us, and bussed tables. What a pleasure to listen as Jim sat with us, pointing out his employees who had been on the streets just the year before. But now they worked hard and served faithfully in his restaurant.

Jim began this project simply by offering a free lunch with

a Bible study, where he talked about the principles of hard work and discipline. Then he developed a fifty-two-week training program to mentor those willing to work in the restaurant business. When they finished the program, they were given a job.

Today Jim is one of the most respected leaders in Charlotte and the best chef in town. He even started the Charlotte Mecklenburg Dream Center, which provides 24/7 care to the neediest in the region—all because he sought the welfare of his city.[8]

 God's people will always find His way to provide His welfare to His children.

These courageous Christians are not satisfied merely to survive in today's Babylon and complain about its problems. They have stepped in to help. They brought God's kingdom to earth in practical ways, prioritizing the welfare of their Babylon.

BY THE PEOPLE, FOR THE PEOPLE

These are only a few examples of what God can do when Christian people decide to be a blessing in their own communities. For you, this might mean transforming the world one student at a time as a teacher or blessing your city one table at a time as a server at a restaurant. Wherever God places you in His kingdom, lead with value right there.

Begin to pray earnestly for your local and national leaders. Cry out to God for His mercy on our nation. And, like Daniel, be willing to confess the sins of the nation and ask for His forgiveness. Then get off your knees and go to work seeking the welfare of America. Lead with value, and be a blessing. Encourage your church to find the needs in your city and meet them—even if you have to press pause on paving the parking lot or buying that new church sign.

Though the cultural narrative may label Christians as "haters" and put us in the lions' dens, may our actions be filled with so much love and carried out with so much excellence that our accusers can find nothing against the way we live, except "with regard to the law of [our] God" (Daniel 6:5). "We give thanks to God always for all of you, making mention of you in our prayers; constantly bearing in mind your work of faith and labor of love and steadfastness of hope in our Lord Jesus Christ in the presence of our God and Father" (1 Thessalonians 1:2–3).

We live in a great nation filled with some awesome people. As a nation, we've rejected God in many ways. But it's still *our* nation, and as Christians, it's our responsibility to seek its welfare. This is a major undertaking because our nation is not just normalizing sin; it's institutionalizing it (codifying into law). But as our catching coach taught us, if we want the right to critique, then we must be willing to step in and help.

We don't believe Jesus is on His throne waving an American flag—or any flag for that matter. But God is a God of people and of nations. He's concerned about both. He loves our nation as He loves each nation, and He seeks its welfare through the love, righteousness, and excellence of a Daniel kind of people.

> God reigns over the nations,
> God sits on His holy throne.
>
> —PSALM 47:8

He made from one man every nation of mankind to live on all the face of the earth, having determined their appointed times and the boundaries of their habitation.

—ACTS 17:26

God has strategically placed you right where you are, in your nation, for such a time as this. So stand with courage, seek the welfare of the city, and watch the transformation.

CHAPTER 17

FACE THE LIONS

"They will fight against you, but they will not overcome you,
for I am with you to deliver you," declares the Lord.
—Jeremiah 1:19

 The bad news is that cowardice is contagious, but the good news is that courage is too!

B ILLY GRAHAM REPORTEDLY ONCE said, "Courage is contagious. When a brave man takes a stand, the spines of others are often stiffened."[1]

In the summer of 480 BC, a great battle between the Greeks and Persians took place. The Persians mounted an imposing army of eighty thousand soldiers under the command of the infamous military legend Xerxes. His elite infantry was not only quite large but very well equipped.

Persia was vastly superior in regard to men and resources. They were going to crush the Greeks and take their land.

When the news reached Greece of the impending invasion,

they mustered everyone they could—four thousand troops. At the heart of their army were three hundred Spartan warriors under the command of their king, Leonidas, whose name meant "son of a lion" or "like a lion." A Spartan warrior had two choices in battle: return home a victor or don't return at all.

They chose to go out and meet the massive Persian army at a narrow mountain pass called Thermopylae. Using a tighter geographic area would allow the Greeks to make the best use of their numbers with Leonidas taking the lead.

When Xerxes arrived and saw the small force of Greek soldiers in position, he believed the army would just surrender, so he waited four days before attacking.

Finally, Xerxes sent an envoy with a message for the Greeks to hand over their company's weapons and submit to him. The story goes that Leonidas sent a message back to Xerxes: "*Molon labe*—'Come and take them!'"[2] Surrender, even with certain death as the outcome, was not an option for these Spartan soldiers. Handing over their weapons without a fight was inconceivable.

Leonidas knew what this meant—Thermopylae would be the place of their death. But they were still willing to face one of the greatest fighting forces ever assembled, even if this meant their final battle.

With unequaled bravery, they held the pass for several days as the Persian force sent wave after wave of troops. A local man showed the Persians a secret passage to encircle the Greeks. As Leonidas realized the plan of attack, he sent the other Greeks home and proposed he and his men would stay and fight. Making this his last stand, he and the infamous three hundred fought valiantly to the death.

Though they lost the battle, the news of their great sacrifice traveled across the Greek countryside. The courage of the Spartans was contagious. Greece ultimately held their ground, and Xerxes, along with all his troops, withdrew back to Persia. The story of Leonidas and his brave soldiers marked Greece forever and made them legends in military history. Today, a monument stands at the site of the great battle as a reminder of their courageous action.[3]

These Spartans faced an enemy they knew would destroy them—a losing battle against an insurmountable enemy. So why did they take their stand? Why would they face the greatest army of all time and refuse to surrender, even after the invading king offered them life?

Greece was *their* kingdom; the women and children they protected were *their* families. They didn't fight because they wanted to. They fought because they had to. They had to protect their nation. They would not cede and live under Persian rule; being subjects to a foreign kingdom was not an option. They believed they had no choice but to defend what was theirs.

Shrinking back before the Enemy of our souls is not an option. Surrendering to what we know isn't right, just so we can keep what we have, is the epitome of cowardice. And while courage is contagious, so is cowardice.

This is why we stressed earlier the importance of making God *your* God. Your faith must be your own—not the faith of your parents, spouse, or pastor, but yours alone. When God is *your* God, *your* Father, and Jesus is *your* Lord, you will stand with courage. And you'll stand for your faith in the same spirit that Leonidas did—"You want my weapons? Come and take 'em!"

Biblical courage flows from a sense of ownership. If we love God, we value His kingdom and His honor more than our own lives. We own it. Courage, then, becomes a natural and irresistible expression of life itself. That kind of courage must fight the good fight of faith—whatever the cost.

 When God is your God and your faith is yours alone, courage will come.

But remember: our battle is vastly different from the Spartans' stand in one crucial way. When the opposing army seems insurmountable, we know that our Lord cannot and will not fail, because He's already won the war (John 16:33; Romans 8:31; 1 Corinthians 15:57; Colossians 2:15).

WHO IS WORTHY?

Another battle took place thousands of years ago. But this was the ultimate battle because our eternal souls were on the line. This conflict, much like the account of Leonidas and the three hundred, was equally hostile. Adam betrayed his Creator, transferred allegiance to the Enemy, and ran in shame (Genesis 4). But God refused to allow this shattering of fellowship to be eternal. So He decided to build a bridge and invited His creation to return home.

But there was one problem. Holy blood was needed to ransom mankind from the Enemy's enslavement (Colossians 1:20; Hebrews 9:22). Humanity's freedom would come at a cost. But who could fulfill this requirement? Only one. The sinless Lion of the tribe of Judah alone qualified to offer His blood as the sacrifice to redeem our souls.

But there's a twist in the story. The Lion had turned into a Lamb—the "Lamb of God who takes away the sin of the world!" (John 1:29).

In His great love for God's precious kids, He fought like a lion by becoming a lamb—a sacrificial lamb—to shed the blood required by the Father to redeem man (Ephesians 1:7). Everyone in heaven knew what this meant. It. Is. Finished! (John 19:30) Blood shed, debt paid, ransom made, redemption done—game over for the Enemy.

This same Lamb is now seated as a Lion on the throne, and we can look to Him for all the courage we need to face the lions in our world today. "Behold, the Lion of the tribe of Judah . . . has conquered" (Revelation 5:5 ESV).

The Lion of Judah has forever defeated the devouring lion of the world.

As Christians, we are lions as well—made even greater because the Lion of Judah lives within us! The way we fight looks different from the way of the lions of this world because it takes the courage of a lion to lay down our lives as lambs. But we are still ferocious and always victorious (1 Corinthians 15:57).

THE LIONHEARTED

Daniel knew His God well, this Lion seated on heaven's throne. So he chose to stand his ground and face the lions of his culture— the physical lions in the den as well as the ideas and arguments of Babylon those lions represented. But because Daniel fought with courage and kept the faith, he overcame them all. "For everyone who has been born of God overcomes the world. And this is the victory that has overcome the world—our faith" (1 John 5:4 ESV).

Daniel didn't back down from his faith, even in the face of certain death. Surrender was not an option. Retreat to safety was nonexistent. God was *his* God, and nothing would change the fact that he was indeed lionhearted—a lion among lions.

TWO PATHS, ONLY ONE WAY

We face lions for different reasons. Some penetrate our defenses because of our own folly while others attack as a part of the normal, spiritual state of this world. "For our struggle is not against flesh and blood, but against the rulers, against the powers, against the world forces of this darkness, against the spiritual forces of wickedness in the heavenly places" (Ephesians 6:12).

Did you know that Daniel wasn't the only man in the Bible to face a physical lion? Below are a few men who faced the beasts as well—two on the path of obedience and two on the path of disobedience.

SAMSON

Samson faced a lion for the wrong reasons. He took an ungodly path to have a relationship with a woman. On the way to her house, a lion attacked him—one he most likely would never have met had he not been going in the wrong direction (Judges 14).

Are you on a similar path, pursuing a relationship outside of God's boundaries for you? If so, turn back now. Sooner or later, a lion will find you on this road, seeking to devour.

The Prophet

Another lion met a young prophet on the road in 1 Kings 13. God sent him to deliver a word of rebuke to Israel's idolatrous king. But God also instructed him not to remain in Israel, but to return to Judah without eating or drinking with anyone. An older prophet invited him for a meal, claiming that God instructed him to do so. But he was lying. The younger prophet believed him—contrary to what God had already told him—and went home with the older prophet to eat. He disobeyed God's original command. As he returned home, a lion killed him along the way.

Has someone else in the faith caused you to doubt, or even abandon, a clear command of God in His Word? Oftentimes, relationships can override or skew our obedience to God's commands.

David

Before he confronted Goliath, David also faced a lion. The beast showed up to devour one of his sheep, but he took him out (1 Samuel 17:34). The attack came as he faithfully fulfilled his calling, so David had the strength to destroy the threat.

Are you faithful in the little things, serving with diligence where God has placed you even when no one is watching? If so, when the lions show up, you'll have the strength to overcome.

BENAIAH

An account of one of David's mighty men—Benaiah, "a doer of great deeds"—tells of all the fearsome enemies he struck down, including one time when he went down into a pit on a snowy day and killed a lion (2 Samuel 23:20). The warrior proactively attacked his enemy; he didn't wait for the beast to stalk him. We believe he went down and killed the lion before the beast could harm anyone else.

Are you allowing a spiritual lion to rip through your family, your church, or your community? It's time to go on the offense, even if the conditions are nasty, and attack before anyone else gets hurt.

Lions hunt along the paths of obedience *and* disobedience. So the question is, which path are you on? You'll encounter them on both roads, so you have to be ready on both roads. But you have the superiority of God's strength behind you only when you walk the path of obedience.

You will cross paths with lions, but the cross of Christ will always overcome.

It's time to get on the right path spiritually. Take courage and get in position to defend your territory or attack your enemy. This is reality. As God's people, we live among lions. But when we walk the path of obedience by faith—like David, Benaiah, and Daniel—God gives us the strength to overcome.

THE FOCUS OF FAITH

We had the privilege to meet Dr. Charles Stanley when we spoke at his church in Atlanta. Outside his office he has a private prayer room where he goes to seek the face of God. We have noticed that *every* spiritual giant we've met has a special place they go to be alone with God. Dr. Stanley often lays flat on his face to pray. What a great example for us.

Inside Dr. Stanley's prayer room hangs a painting of Daniel in the lions' den. The lions are prowling around, looking as if they will devour him at any moment. Bones lie scattered on the ground, the remains of others who had met their death there. The picture gave us a sense of the gravity of Daniel's experience.

But Daniel's posture was the image we'll never forget. He was standing with his back to the lions, clasping his hands gently and staring up in the direction of heaven. He was focusing on God, not the circumstances. Even in the lions' den, he kept his customs and stood by faith, not fear, just as he had done from his first day in Babylon.

Daniel was able to face the lions of his culture and the lions in the den, because he focused on the Lion who was seated on the throne of heaven. Daniel knew God could shut the beasts' mouths, but even if He chose not to (as his friends told Nebuchadnezzar), he was willing to face the den (Daniel 3:18). Why? God was *his* God.

While we don't know exactly what Daniel did when he was in the den, we know that he went into the den armed with faith in God, and he came out with the same faith—never wavering.

STANDING FIRM IN THE STORM

As we close this final chapter, we want you to remember Dr. Erwin Lutzer's answer when we asked him if God was going to judge America. "The question is not, 'Will God judge America?' The question is, 'What does faithfulness look like in the midst of God's judgment?'"[4]

We could never shake that conversation. His question stuck with us, burning in our hearts. That's when God drew us to the book of Daniel and began to speak to our spirits.

This book is our answer to Dr. Lutzer's crucial question. We felt called to write a charge to God's people to get ready. And now is the time. We must prepare to live with conviction, commitment, and courage, just like Daniel.

He was prepared for life in Babylon; he was prepared for living among lions, having readied himself while still in Judah, his homeland. He got close to God before the storm hit and took the time to deepen his walk with God.

We're betting that in some of those very trying moments alone under Nebuchadnezzar's and Darius's reigns, Daniel must have prayed something like this:

LORD GOD, THANK YOU FOR GETTING ME READY BACK in Judah, for making me strong, for challenging me *there* to prepare for life *here*. Without You warning me, inspiring me, showing me, and drawing me to Yourself, I would not have survived here, much less had the impact You made on this nation through me. Thank You that You didn't let me wait to get to Babylon, in the midst of the mess, to decide

to walk deeply with You. You readied me back at home for
the battles here in Babylon!

We wrote this book because we see a storm coming, a cultural storm of pressure—and perhaps even persecution—that
will require miraculous courage in the face of adversity. But here's
the good news: boldness opens the door to the miraculous. Just
as Daniel's boldness led to the closing of the lions' mouths and
David's courage paved a way for the giant to fall, we, too, might
see the miraculous if we stand boldly.

 Boldness opens the door to the miraculous.

Maybe you see the storm too. No, there may not be a pagan
army headed this way to take us all captive, but a new pagan
nation is approaching, nonetheless, from within. Sure, we can
turn our backs and ignore the invasion, but this won't change the
fact that we are living in a *very different country* right now than the
one we were living in just a few years ago.

So we wrote this book to help you get ready to stand with
courage ahead of the approaching storm.

Our Christian brothers and sisters are being thrown into
a cultural lions' den as the battle lines are clearly drawn. Like
Leonidas and the three hundred soldiers, we must decide this is
not a political or cultural war but rather one for the souls of our
children. We must stand in the gap at our own Thermopylae to
protect against the coming onslaught.

In the history of our faith, the gospel of Jesus Christ has never been on the defense, rather always, *always* on the offense—on the march, on the move, pressing on, and advancing on the gates of hell.

The gospel is good news. And here is some very good news for you right now. Though we are living in an ever-declining, post-Christian culture, our God is at work. He is saving, redeeming, transforming, healing, delivering, rescuing, and bringing hope, love, grace, mercy, joy, goodness, and compassion to all who will call upon the name of Jesus Christ.

In our generation the time of purifying, cleansing, and refining is at hand.

This is the time to prepare.

We pray you grow in wisdom.

We pray you will decide to live a transformed life in order to transform your world with

      conviction that transforms your heart,

         commitment that transforms your lifestyle,

            courage that transforms your world—courage to

               stand firm and be found living among lions.

BENHAM PRINCIPLES

1. Pressure is feeling the push of culture to stray from our faith. Persecution is feeling the pain of choices made as we stand for our faith.

2. Today we must reach out and resist. Reach out with compassion to people trapped in sin, but resist with courage the agenda to impose that sin.

3. The same rising tide of evil that makes cowards run makes champions rise.

4. God's love is unconditional, but God's mercy is conditioned upon our repentance.

5. If persecution comes to America, perseverance in Christ will reinvigorate believers and reinforce the body of Christ.

6. Christians are to be the chocolate chips in the cookie dough of culture. We are to *mix in*, not *blend in*—we keep our form, remaining completely distinct and separate—yet we should make the batch great!

7. Trusting God's promises and following God's practices will bring God's promotion.

8. God has called us to be His faithful messengers even if His message is not popular.

9. When our level of conviction matches God's call, courage can crush any crisis.

10. We grow much more through battling our burdens than banking our blessings.

11. Readiness is realized before the roar is heard.

12. Never focus on fame by the world's standards but on faithfulness by God's standards. This is where heavenly success will always be found.

13. If we want to know who we are, we need a reference point outside of ourselves. This is where Christianity has the answer. How do we know who we are? Our Creator tells us.

14. Knowing our true identity breeds conviction, and conviction fuels our actions.

15. True satisfaction for the Christian is not found in promotion or profit, increase or influence, but in his identity as a child of God.

16. As Christians, we should find our identity in who we are, not what we do. Yet what we do will always flow out of who we are. This is the key to inside-out living.

17. To live among lions, who you are must come from who He is.

18. Outward affiliation never equals inward transformation.

19. The world wants us to *con*form. But God wants us to *trans*form so we can make a difference in this world.

20. Kids need to hear this today: if they learn to say no now, when their bodies say yes, then it will be much easier for them to courageously say no later, when their culture demands they say yes.

21. Renouncing Satan's lies and replacing them with God's truth brings renewal.

22. Internal transformation precedes genuine external transformation. The river of holiness always flows from the inside out.

23. A biblical worldview takes your faith and makes it a lens through which you filter all of life so you can live faithfully.

24. If you straddle the fence, you'll tear the seat of your pants.

25. With a biblical worldview, separating our lives and the surrounding culture into sacred and secular compartments is impossible.

26. For America to return to the blessing of her heritage, we must return to a biblical worldview.

27. Those who bow in reverence to God and leave the results to Him will become relevant in His time, in His way.

28. Christians should focus on the Spirit, doing what pleases God, before they focus on strategy, doing what makes sense to man.

29. Christians should never focus on the frowns of people but on the face of God.

30. The same boiling water that hardens the egg softens the carrot. Don't focus on the temperature of the water but on the substance of what's in the water.

31. A position of influence with man will never compare with the pathway to inheritance with God.

32. To be transformers for God in the world, our internal convictions must be cemented by external commitments.

33. What God has done for us is easy to talk about, but what God requires of us is more challenging to discuss.

34. Daniel was committed to living within the boundaries because he was surrendered to the Boundary Giver.

35. God's boundary lines are in place for our protection. The Enemy tells us these are unnecessary restrictions keeping us from having fun when they are actually necessary restraints keeping us from being harmed.

36. Faithfulness in what God has called you to do, right where He's called you to be, is the foundation for excellence.

37. Excellence is not a destination but a destiny—being all that God designed us to be for His glory.

38. Faithfulness leads to excellence, which opens the door for influence.

39. Faithfulness in your work will lead to promotion while faithfulness in your walk will lead to persecution.

40. If we want the transformational life of Jesus to flow through us into our world, we cannot do it apart from a commitment to His Word.

41. Commit to consistent time in God's Word, and the motivation will follow. In time your heart will catch up with your habit.

42. Without diligence in God's Word, there will be no discernment—and without discernment, there will be no sense of direction.

43. Wrap your beliefs around the Bible. Never wrap the Bible around your beliefs.

44. Powerful prayers are not centered on petitions but on praise.

45. Prayer is a two-way conversation to connect and communicate with our Father. It's not about getting things from God—it's about getting to God and experiencing intimacy with Him.

46. We are to focus not on getting answers to our prayers but on growing with the God who answers them.

47. Maintaining a disposition of expectancy will open our eyes and ears to see and hear God when others don't.

48. If you don't wait for the Lord, you may still have wings—but more like a hummingbird, you work a lot harder and fly a lot lower.

49. Whether in promotion or persecution, God's presence empowers the humbled heart.

50. When gratitude replaces selfishness, humility replaces pride.

51. Humility is the first step toward healing. And healing—both personally and in community—is a transformational process. Humility opens the door for transformation to begin.

52. God's kids + Humility = Power

53. To be powerful purifiers, we must first be personally pure.

54. Mixing a love for God with a love for the world is the quickest way to turn a hero into a zero, a warrior into a wimp.

55. The temptation is to crawl off the altar when the heat turns up. But if we stay on the altar, constantly sacrificing our own thoughts, attitudes, actions, and motives, purity becomes not a work we do but a way we live.

56. If you desire a life of purity, then you must embrace the storms that purify.

57. To live among lions today, we must first embrace the storm that purifies—pursuing purity on the inside so we can live purely on the outside.

58. When we have been purified by God's flame on the inside, we will be untouched by man's furnace on the outside.

59. Soft heart + Hard head = Courage

60. God loves all people, but He does not love all ideas.

61. A Christian boldly resists the ideas exalted against the knowledge of God but reaches out with compassion to the people who hold them.

62. The softer our hearts grow toward God, the harder our heads should grow toward evil—in our own lives and in the culture around us.

63. Courageous transformers confront culture with hard heads because with soft hearts they love the people in it.

64. For our courage to be displayed, we must show up, stand strong, and stay put!

65. The resolve to stand is our responsibility; the result of our stand is God's.

66. We are not issue fighters but kingdom advancers. Divine purpose drives our passion.

67. If persecutors can't get you to bow to *their* god, they'll try to force you not to bow to yours.

68. Laws may threaten our liberty but never our love for the Lord.

69. God's confirmation will come down when our courage rises up.

70. Even when our rights are not recognized, we have a responsibility to do what's right.

71. Keeping our gaze on the grace of heaven keeps our grip off the gifts of men.

72. The moment we grab the goodies of the world, we give up the greatness of the kingdom.

73. Focusing on the reward of heaven's King brings the courage to speak truth to earth's kings.

74. The parades of man will never match the peace of God's mission.

75. The courage that transforms a nation seeks to bless the nation even when people refuse that blessing.

76. God designed us to be His conduits, not cul-de-sacs, with blessings flowing through us, not stopping with us.

77. God's people will always find His way to provide His welfare to His children.

78. When God is your God and your faith is yours alone, courage will come.

79. The Lion of Judah has forever defeated the devouring lion of the world.

80. You will cross paths with lions, but the cross of Christ will always overcome.

81. Boldness opens the door to the miraculous.

ACKNOWLEDGMENTS

T O THOSE WHO HELPED us complete this project—sometimes it felt like a tennis match as we volleyed back and forth . . . again and again. Through it all, we were able to craft the content into this book. And, in the process, we sharpened one another a good bit too!

Dr. Bob Gladstone, our good friend and spiritual mentor. This book didn't happen without your help. Thanks for teaching us through the years on the life of Daniel. Your wisdom into his life and the way you live it out is a powerful testimony that has helped us along our journey. You're a stud—just plain and simple (and you did a great job as the pastor in the movie *War Room* too!).

Robert Noland, our buddy and thought organizer. You have ninja skills—some call those talents—you use as tools, not toys. Thanks for your faithfulness to this project and for your incredibly high professional and personal standards. Your ministry to men—the Knights Code—and your help with this book have greatly impacted us.

Dr. Michael Brown, our friend and elder in the faith. You

are a fearless warrior filled with the compassion of Christ. What a powerful combination! Thank you for your investment in our lives, your prophetic voice in culture, and the message of Daniel that you live every day. You've chosen to keep your windows open—by life or by death. We're with you every step of the way.

Jason Jimenez, our brother from another mother. You know the Bible like the back of your hand, and the fact that you're younger than us makes us jealous—but we know we're not supposed to be. Your insights on how to gain a biblical worldview have given us new eyes to see God's Word. Thanks for your help with that.

And, of course, to Momma and Poppa Bear (that's Mom and Dad). Dad, when you read through our initial drafts, you walked into our office and spoke to the warrior in us to write from the heart—to hold nothing back. Well, we did what you said and hope it works. Mom, you are always so encouraging and still think we can do no wrong (at least you're hopeful). Thanks for all the eggs and grits. We love you.

Last but not least, thank you to the two ladies who keep us ticking—our beautiful wives, Lori and Tori. You are the halves that make us whole. You are the unsung heroes of this project, so we wanted to say as loud as we could, *"Thank you—we love you!"*

NOTES

Introduction: God's People in a *Very* Different Country

1. Mrs. Barronelle Stutzman, personal conversation with authors, October 16, 2014.
2. Aaron and Melissa Klein, personal conversation with authors, September 26, 2014.
3. Kelvin Cochran, e-mail to authors, November 2, 2014.
4. Kim Davis, personal conversation with authors, September 8, 2015.
5. John F. Walvoord, "Early Life of Daniel in Babylon," Bible.org, accessed October 18, 2015, https://bible.org/seriespage/1-early -life-daniel-babylon.
6. Flip Benham, paraphrase of Matthew Henry, *Commentary on the Whole Bible*, Amos 5, BibleStudyTools.com, accessed June 4, 2015, http://www.biblestudytools.com/commentaries/matthew-henry -complete/amos/5.html.

Authors' Note I: America: A Nation Changed

1. Leslie Jordan, lecture at Human Rights Campaign Dinner, Charlotte Convention Center, Charlotte, North Carolina, February 23, 2007.
2. Dr. Michael Brown, personal conversation with authors, December 12, 2007.

3. Engel v. Vitale, 370 U.S. 421 (1962).

4. School District of Abington Township, Pennsylvania v. Schempp, 374 U.S. 203 (1963).

5. Roe v. Wade, 410 U.S. 113 (1973).

6. Stone v. Graham, 449 U.S. 39 (1980).

7. Planned Parenthood of Southeastern Pennsylvania et al. v. Casey, Governor of Pennsylvania, et al, Certiorari to the United States Court of Appeals for the Third Circuit, 91-744 (1992).

8. Obergefell v. Hodges, Director, Ohio Department of Health, et al. Certiorari to the United States of Appeals for the Sixth Circuit, 14-556 (2015).

9. James Dobson, "High Court on Verge of Destroying the Family," WND Commentary, May 3, 2015, http://www.wnd.com/2015/05/high-court-on-verge-of-destroying-the-family/.

10. Elton Trueblood, quoted in Leonard Ravenhill, *Sodom Had No Bible* (Pensacola, FL: Christian Life Books, 1971), 17.

11. Leonard Ravenhill, "Weeping Between the Porch and the Altar—Part 1," Messages, Ravenhill.org, accessed June 24, 2015, http://www.ravenhill.org/weeping1.htm. Copyright 1994 by Leonard Ravenhill, Lindale, Texas, http://www.ravenhill.org. Used with permission.

12. Donald Knoblet, e-mail to authors, May 20, 2015.

13. David Platt, *Counter Culture* (Carol Stream, IL: Tyndale House Publishers, 2015), 21.

14. Dr. Erwin Lutzer, personal conversation with authors, September 15, 2013.

Authors' Note 2: Babylon

1. Easton's Bible Dictionary, s.v. "Daniel," Bible Study Tools, accessed October 18, 2015, http://www.biblestudytools.com/dictionary/daniel/.

2. The Jefferson Monticello, "Spurious Quotations," Monticello and the Thomas Jefferson Foundation, accessed June 25, 2015, https://www.monticello.org/site/jefferson/matters-style-swim-currentquotation.

3. Studies in Revelation, "Babylon as Seen in Scripture," Bible.org, accessed June 22, 2015, https://bible.org/seriespage/23-babylon-seen-scripture-introduction-rev-17-18.

4. John F. Walvoord, "Early Life of Daniel in Babylon," Bible.org, accessed October 18, 2015, https://bible.org/seriespage/1-early-life-daniel-babylon.

5. These are the Google search results as of July 1, 2015.

6. Patricia Cummings, "The Cherokee Indian Youth's Rite of Passage," Examiner.com, accessed June 5, 2015, http://www.examiner.com/article/the-cherokee-indian-youth-s-rite-of-passage.

Chapter 2: Know Your Identity

1. Russell Goldman, "Here's a List of 58 Gender Options for Facebook Users," ABCNews, February 13, 2014, http://abcnews.go.com/blogs/headlines/2014/02/heres-a-list-of-58-gender-options-for-facebook-users/.

2. Michael L. Brown, *Answering Jewish Objections to Jesus, Vol. 5: Traditional Jewish Objections* (San Francisco: Purple Pomegranate Productions, 2010), 175, citing John H. Walton, Victor H. Matthews, and Mark W. Chavalas, *The IVP Bible Background Commentary: Old Testament* (Downers Grove, IL: InterVarsity Press, 2000), 731.

3. David and Jason Benham's *Whatever the Cost* interview by *Fox & Friends* cast, February 10, 2015, *Fox & Friends* (Fox News Network).

4. Frank Newport, "Seven in 10 Americans Are Very or Moderately Religious," December 4, 2012, Gallup, http://www.gallup.com/poll/159050/seven-americans-moderately-religious.aspx.

Chapter 3: Think Your Identity

1. Merriam-Webster Online, s.v. "renounce," accessed October 16, 2015, http://www.merriam-webster.com/dictionary/renounce.

Chapter 4: Build Your Worldview

1. Charles Colson and Nancy Pearcey, *How Now Shall We Live?* (Carol Stream, IL: Tyndale House Publishers, 1999), 14–15.
2. Ibid., 16.
3. Rick Johnson, *The Power of a Man* (Grand Rapids: Revell, 2009), 153.
4. Edwin Percy Whipple ed., *The Great Speeches and Orations of Daniel Webster* (Washington, DC: Beard Books, 2001), 51.
5. Steve Deace, *Rules for Patriots: How Conservatives Can Win Again* (Franklin, TN: Post Hill Press, 2014), 32.

Chapter 5: Choose Reverence

1. Glen R. Martin, *Prevailing Worldviews of Western Society Since 1500* (Newton, MA: Triangle Publishing Services, 2006), 58–59.

Chapter 6: Draw the Line

1. Composer unknown, attributed to S. Sundar Singh, "I Have Decided to Follow Jesus," public domain.
2. Jesse Johnson, "Why We Sing 'I Have Decided to Follow Jesus,'" The Cripplegate, May 29, 2013, http://thecripplegate.com/why -we-sing-i-have-decided-to-follow-jesus/.
3. Tremper Longman III, *The NIV Application Commentary: Daniel* (Grand Rapids: Zondervan, 1999), 48.
4. Hayim H. Donin, *To Be a Jew: A Guide to Jewish Observance in Contemporary Life* (New York: Basic Books, 1991), 99.
5. Oswald Chambers, *My Utmost for His Highest*, December 1 entry (Grand Rapids: Discovery House, 1992).
6. Dr. James Dobson, "Do Kids Really Want Boundaries," Dr. James Dobson's Family Talk, accessed June 28, 2015, http://drjamesdobson .org/Solid-Answers/Answers?a=023fcea0-f871-4f55-9427-9d37920c4234.

Chapter 7: Live with Excellence

1. Sports-Reference: College Football, s.v. "Lou Holtz," accessed August 19, 2015, http://www.sports-reference.com/cfb/coaches /lou-holtz-1.html.

2. Lou Holtz, keynote speech at Lou's Lads Annual Dinner, South Bend, Indiana, September 4, 2014.

3. Bible Hub, *Strong's Concordance*, s.v. "tektón," accessed June 9, 2015, http://biblehub.com/greek/5045.htm.

Chapter 8: Read God's Word

1. Ray Vander Laan, "Follow the Rabbi," lectures at Focus on the Family, October 5, 2008, http://oneinjesus.info/2008/10/ray-vander-laans-follow-the-rabbi-lectures/.

2. John R. W. Stott, "The Wisdom of John R. W. Stott," King's Meadow Study Center, accessed November 12, 2015, https://www.kingsmeadow.com/wp/the-wisdom-of-john-r-w-stott/.

3. Charles Colson and Nancy Pearcey, *How Now Shall We Live?* (Wheaton, IL: Tyndale, 1999), 16.

Chapter 9: The Power of Prayer

1. Lysa TerKeurst, acceptance speech for Book Impact Award, 2015 K-LOVE Fan Awards, Grand Ole Opry, Nashville, Tennessee, June 5, 2015.

2. Elisabeth Elliott, *Keep a Quiet Heart* (Ann Arbor, MI: Vine Books, 1995), 215.

3. Oswald Chambers, *My Utmost for His Highest*, February 7 entry (Grand Rapids: Discovery House, 1992).

4. E. M. Bounds, *Power Through Prayer* (Norcross, GA: Trinity Press, 2012), 10.

Chapter 10: The Strength of Humility

1. *Webster's American Dictionary of the English Language*, 1828 edition, s.v. "humility," accessed November 6, 2015, http://webstersdictionary1828.com/Home?word=Humility.

2. Chip Ingram, *Spiritual Simplicity: Doing Less, Loving More* (New York: Howard Books, 2013), 59.

Chapter 11: The Power of Purity

1. "Study Shows Lightning Adds to Ozone Level," Texas A&M University, public release: March 19, 2003, in EurekAlert!, American Association for the Advancement of Science, http://www.eurekalert.org/pub_releases/2003-03/tau-ssl031903.php.

Part III: Courage that Transforms My World

1. Elizabeth Rundle Charles, *Chronicles of the Schönberg-Cotta Family*, vol. 1 (London: T. Nelson and Sons, 1876), 276.
2. *Braveheart*, original screenplay by Randall Wallace, 1995.
3. Dr. Martin Luther King Jr., MLK Selma Speeches 1965, YouTube video, 3:20, posted by "dougcoops," March 8, 2012, https://www.youtube.com/watch?v=0On19DRA2fU.

Chapter 12: A Hard Head and a Soft Heart

1. Oswald Chambers, *My Utmost for His Highest*, June 28 entry (Grand Rapids: Discovery House, 1992).
2. Read more about Gabe Lyons at qideas.org, http://qideas.org/contributors/gabe-lyons/.

Chapter 13: Let It Be Known

1. David and Jason Benham, interview by Steve Doocy, July 10, 2014, *Fox & Friends* (Fox News).
2. Matthew Henry, "Commentary on the Whole Bible, Daniel, Chapter 3," Christian Classics Ethereal Library, accessed August 23, 2015, http://www.ccel.org/ccel/henry/mhc4.Dan.iv.html.
3. David George, *The Daily Thought Shaker* (Bloomington, IN: WestBow Press, 2014), 18.

Chapter 16: Seek the Welfare of the City

1. *Webster's American Dictionary of the English Language*, 1828 edition, s.v. "welfare," accessed November 6, 2015, http://webstersdictionary1828.com/Dictionary/welfare.

2. Tony Evans, *Kingdom Man: Every Man's Destiny, Every Woman's Dream* (Carol Stream, IL: Tyndale House Publishers, 2015), 150.

3. Thom Schultz, "The Shocking Truth of Church Budgets," Church Leaders, accessed June 3, 2015, http://www.churchleaders.com /pastors/pastor-blogs/169385-the-shocking-truth-of-church -budgets.html.

4. Paul Arnsberger, Melissa Ludlum, Margaret Riley, Mark Stanton, "A History of the Tax-Exempt Sector: An SOI Perspective, Internal Revenue Service," Internal Revenue Service, accessed June 28, 2015, http://www.irs.gov/pub/irs-soi/tehistory.pdf.

5. Billy Graham Evangelistic Association, "Helping Children of Inmates in Charleston, NC 1965," YouTube video, 5:18, posted by "Billy Graham Evangelistic Association," July 20, 2013, https:// youtu.be/lmm9fTNAltc.

6. For more information visit proverbs226.org.

7. "Truth and Mercy Pro-Life Ministries' Mission," Truth and Mercy Pro-Life Ministries, accessed July 2, 2015, http://www .truthandmercyprolife.org.

8. "Our Mission," The King's Kitchen, accessed July 2, 2015, http:// kingskitchen.org/mission/.

Chapter 17: Face the Lions

1. Billy Graham, quoted in Allan Taylor, *Sunday School in HD: Sharpening the Focus on What Makes Your Church Healthy* (Nashville: B&H Publishing Group, 2009), 175.

2. Justin Marozzi, *The Way of Herodotus: Travels with the Man Who Invented History* (Philadelphia, PA: Da Capo Press, 2008), 199.

3. "Leonidas, the King of Sparta," Greeka.com, The Greek Islands Specialists, accessed October 19, 2015, http://www.greeka.com /greece-history/famous-people/leonidas.htm.

4. Dr. Erwin Lutzer, personal conversation with authors, September 15, 2013.

ABOUT THE AUTHORS

D AVID AND JASON BENHAM are former professional baseball players, nationally acclaimed entrepreneurs, and bestselling authors of the book *Whatever the Cost*. The twin brothers' business success earned them a reality show with HGTV, set to air during the 2014 fall season. Due to their commitment to biblical values, however, the show was abruptly canceled. The Benhams immediately found themselves in the midst of a cultural firestorm, but they refused to back down and decided to stand and fight for what they believe.

The brothers' first company was recognized as one of *Inc.* magazine's Fastest Growing Private Companies, and they have been awarded Ernst & Young's Entrepreneur of the Year Finalists, *Wall Street Journal*'s Top Real Estate Professionals, and *Business Leader Media*'s Top 50 Entrepreneurs. They were also named *Franchise 500*'s Top New Franchise.

Appearing on CNN, Fox News, TheBlaze, ABC's *Nightline*, *Good Morning America*, and other media, the Benhams continue to stand up for what they believe and encourage others to do the same.

Both David and Jason are happily married, and their families live on the same street in Charlotte, North Carolina. Their wives, Lori and Tori, homeschool their combined nine children and are passionate about serving in their community.

Follow David and Jason on Twitter:
@DavidDBenham
@JasonBBenham
Visit their website, BenhamBrothers.com,
like them on Facebook/BenhamBrothers, and
follow them on Instagram/BenhamBrothers.